BOOKKEEPING
AND TAX PREPARATION

Start and Build a Prosperous
Bookkeeping, Tax, and Financial
Services Business

BOOKKEEPING
AND TAX PREPARATION

Start and Build a Prosperous
Bookkeeping, Tax, and Financial
Services Business

GORDON P. LEWIS

ACTON CIRCLE

...eparation: Start and Build a Prosperous ...nancial Services Business

Published by: Acton Circle Publishing Company
                   P. O. Box 1564
                   Ukiah, California 95482

Cover design by Jeanne H. Koelle, Koelle & Gillette.
Office floor plan by Irene Stein.

Trademarked names are used throughout this book. Rather than put a trademark symbol at every occurrence of a trademarked name, we state that we are using the names in an editorial fashion and to the benefit of the trademark owner with no intention to infringe the trademark. No such use of any trademark or trade name is intended to connote an endorsement or other affiliation with the book.

Disclaimer

This book provides information about the subject matter covered. It is sold with the understanding that the publisher and author are not engaged in giving legal, accounting, or other professional services or advice in the book. A reader who requires legal or other expert assistance should seek the services of the appropriate competent professional.

Published in 1996.

10 9 8 7 6 5 4 3

Publisher's Cataloging in Publication

Lewis, Gordon P , 1953-

    Bookkeeping and tax preparation: start and build a prosperous bookkeeping, tax, and financial services business / Gordon P. Lewis.—Ukiah, Calif.: Acton Circle, 1996.

    179 p.;   ill.; cm.
    Includes index.

    ISBN 0-9639371-7-0

1. Small business management. 2. New business enterprises—Management. I. Title.

    HD62.7 .L674   1996   658.11

    Library of Congress Catalog Card Number 95-83817

*To the legions of small-business
entrepreneurs who are the
rank, file, and esprit of
people's capitalism.*

Recognition and Appreciation

Ultimately this book's completion was due to the steady support of my long-suffering, always cheerful, almost irreplaceable assistant, Yvonne Hadsell, to whom—as for all the business's achievements—I extend a full measure of my gratitude.

Further, I am indebted to and very grateful for the generosity of the devoted public servants in the Internal Revenue Service who responded beyond our expectations with research and material assistance for the book. A few of them include Jodie Patterson, of the IRS Media Relations Division; John J. Dopkin, Chief of the Tax Forms Development Branch; and Elta Hutson, of the Western Area Distribution Center. Thanks to them we were lucky enough to use the resources of the Summer 1987 issue of *IRS Service* for our thumbnail sketch of the Service's history, which appears randomly throughout this book. We also relied on a history of internal revenue from 1862 to 1963, *The American Way in Taxation*, edited by Lillian Doris and published by Prentice-Hall in 1963.

I extend sincere thanks to my colleagues who responded to our request to use their advertising and their business-card design as examples of how to publicize right. They are Susan Chandler of Chandler Financial Services in Santa Fe, New Mexico; Mel Cutler in Salinas, California; Ernest Dubnicoff, EA, of CRT Associates in Cardiff, California; Chris Jensen of Jensen & Novacic, Inc.; Helen Kochenderfer of

Kochenderfer Business and Accounting Services; Diane Lavin of Karkiainen and Lavin; Sten B. Mattsson, EA; and Jo Rogers of Rogers & Associates—all in San Francisco. Thanks go also to Don Wehr at Office Furniture U.S.A. in Santa Rosa, California, for the opportunity to use his company's great can't-miss classified ad. I am extremely grateful to Bonnie L. Graas who patiently, and often with pointed humor, transcribed my taped thoughts on this subject into readable pages. I also thank my publisher and editor, Dori and Tom Anderson, who got me started on the project and steered it into print.

Finally, this book would have been much poorer without the scrutiny and comments of my peers, Judy Luchsinger, John Robertson, CPA, V. James Sligh, CPA, and Kathy Wallis, all of whom graciously reviewed and improved early drafts of the manuscript. Last (but not least if I ever want to hear the end of it) I thank my brother Steve Lewis, former journalism professor and wordsmith extraordinaire, for his astute review and burnishing of the book's penultimate draft.

Lakeport, California, 1996   *G.P.L.*

Contents

Contents

It's the free enterprise system at its best. The harder and smarter you work, the more money you make. It depends only on how far you want to expand and extend the business.

1

An Overview

ABOUT seven years ago I took a financial blow so serious that I lost everything I owned except my sense of humor and a few personal effects. I wound up owing more money than many people make in 10 years. It was a catastrophe. It wiped me out and handed me a very bleak future indeed. Worst of all, it wasn't even my fault! But there it was: my worst fears realized.

Luckily, I worked then as I do now at a profession with a great potential for monetary reward as well as personal satisfaction—bookkeeping and tax preparation.

Today the disaster is well behind me. I got over it by building on the professional skills I had acquired and shaping them into a business that has erased my past reversal and now supports a very comfortable way of life.

You don't have to endure the worst, however, to make the most of this business. That's why I wrote this book. It's for bookkeepers and tax preparers who want to set up on their own but have questions about how to get the business running on a day-to-day basis, avoid its pitfalls, and take it as far as they want. It's a chance to pass along my experience in how to develop, use, manage, and market the necessary skills, so that your services will be in high demand and you can prosper as I have. I also wrote the book to save you the trouble of reinventing a number of wheels—always a laborious and costly process. I firmly believe in getting as much cheap knowledge as possible before going out to get a lot of expensive experience. So here it is, a volume of cheap knowledge: the straight stuff and my big-ticket wheel-making stories.

How I Got Into the Business

I was attracted to this business when I finally understood who I was. I'm a guy who enjoys working intensely for short periods of time. I usually do poorly if I have to work intensely or even steadily over a long stretch. What attracts me to the tax part of this business is that I can work very hard for four or five months of the year and have a significant amount of time off after that. I consider this a major benefit.

Before I prepared taxes and did people's books I was a civil rights investigator in San Francisco for the Office of Civil Rights, which was a part of the former Department of Health, Education, and Welfare. I was a bureaucrat and I was miserable. I didn't like the bureaucracy. I didn't like the work I was doing or the people I worked for. One night when I was watching TV I saw an advertisement for the H&R Block School of Tax Preparation. I took the course and worked for Block for a year. I had a liking and knack for the business and found out that my friends would pay me money to help with their taxes. Then I went to work for a small accounting firm in San Francisco and got a little more experience. After a year I decided to strike out on my own as a tax preparer.

The Advantages

If you are like me, self employment in bookkeeping and tax preparation has a lot to offer. First, you are not an employee, you are the boss. That means you are responsible for your own decisions but at least *you* make the decisions and can follow through on them. As far as the business allows, and the more you learn about it, you can structure your own time, working habits, work environment, and even to some extent where and how you live.

It has the advantage also of giving personal control over the upper limit of how much money you make. It lets you work toward a higher profit potential and depends only on how far you decide to expand and extend the business. "Expand" and "extend" mean different things. I will discuss them later.

A successful practice will produce gross revenues of between $60,000 and $100,000 a year, with about 40 to 45 percent net to the proprietor before taxes. Those sums are for a sole practitioner, and it is possible to earn much more than that. It's the free enterprise system at its best. The harder and smarter you want to work, the more money you can make. That has a real allure for those of us who don't make the world's finest employees.

These income figures, incidentally, are based on my experience in a small-town practice. You can be in a rural, suburban, urban area—or almost anywhere. With electronics, computers, data processing, and fax-modems you could theoretically work in Siberia if you chose to and could find the clients. We will see later about finding the clients.

Money for which no receipt has been taken is not to be included in the accounts.

—Code of Hammurabi (ca. 2000 B.C.)

Also, bookkeeping and tax preparation are a core industry and can provide very steady and satisfying employment for those of us who enjoy the work. Today especially, small businesses must be competitive simply in order to survive if not succeed, and competitiveness has always required a good set of books. Profitable businesses keep good books; unprofitable ones may have poor books or none at all. Many small-business people lack the understanding, inclination, time, money, personnel—or some combination of them—to keep their own books. I read of one businessman who couldn't keep his checkbook balanced, so he kept two accounts. He used one until his monthly statement came in. Then he switched to the other one. Some still scribble a few numbers on the back of envelopes and hope for the best. Usually it comes to the worst, and they fail.

A survey of business people in a large eastern city in the 1950s showed that 15 percent of businesses kept only files of their bills. Forty-nine percent kept some kind of single-entry books, and only eight percent kept a full set of double-entry books. The survey estimated that 43 percent needed bookkeeping services. Those figures probably have not changed much since the late fifties. If scholastic test scores mean anything, people are probably no more skilled at figuring than they ever were.

Also, with the steady increase of tax laws and regulations at all levels of government, there is a constant if not rising demand for qualified people to keep business records and prepare tax reports for individuals as well as businesses. Good bookkeepers and tax preparers are in a secure, if not growth, industry. Doing well at it, however, requires not only a sound training in bookkeeping, but a grasp of taxation and tax law, accounting principles, commercial law, finance, and insurance. You need good communication skills in order to write and speak clearly to clients. To make the venture a success, however, a bookkeeper and tax preparer needs business skills equal, if not superior, to those of any other small entrepreneur.

On Your Own - Is It for You?

There are two kinds of people in this world: Those who are good and desirable employees, and rest of us who aren't. Through some quirk of character or pure cussedness, we find ourselves unable to work for other people, but we do like working *with* other people. Anyway, that is what I decided about myself; so my "unemployability" and the pleasure I get from my work is how I got into the business and why I stay.

Before striking out on your own, you will ask, "Do I want to take on the responsibility of working for myself?" "Do I really have to be the boss and call the shots?" No, not necessarily. This occupation can also provide an income supplement. It can be adapted and developed to any size; so that anyone looking for additional income each month could handle one or two accounts and bring in an extra few hundred dollars a month.

Still, knowing the tricks and traps of the trade can save a lot of anguish even for a part-timer. Remember that "striking out" can be taken two ways. Don't worry about it. My main message is to be honest with yourself. Don't underrate your capabilities, but be realistic and don't expect to leap into a brand new career and make $100,000 in the first year.

Let's assume, for example, that right now you are working as a book-keeper for $26,000 a year. If you can get 15 clients at an average fee of $150 per month, your total annual receipts would be $27,000 per year. The extra $1,000 a year alone would probably not justify quitting your present job and setting up on your own. If you could get 20 clients at

$150 per month, the year's receipts would be $36,000, at which point the prospect of going independent might begin to sound attractive. Remember that gross earnings have to cover not only your overhead and salary, including comparable mandated benefits, but must make a profit, too.

Here are some preliminary considerations. First, you need to determine whether there are enough clients out there who want your services. If so, you need to estimate how long it will take you to build up that client base. You need to know what the costs are of surviving until you reach break-even. That means calculating your operating expenses before taking the fateful step. Will the $10,000 above your current salary cover all your expenses? If your calculations show they will, and you take that step, you have demonstrated the entrepreneur's first characteristic: risk taking. Leaving a secure job, no matter how bad it seems, means risking money, other assets, time, and possibly your reputation. It is a big step. As I said, however, you don't have to take it all at once.

An alternative is to supplement current income by working part-time on weekends or evenings, with one or two accounts. It can bring in that extra $200 to $400 a month without jeopardizing a current job. Also, established bookkeepers and tax practitioners may want part-time help. Approaching them allows you to learn what the business is like and to begin to make contacts in it. If you have a full-time practice in mind, how will your proposed boss feel about you as a potential competitor? That's hard to predict. As a colleague you could become a partner or a good referral for excess work. There is a lot of reliance on networking and load-sharing in this business. There has to be.

You Do It All - A One-Person Band

As boss you have to do the work and also run the business. You do *all* the work, the menial and the glamorous. I was tickled when I found this out soon after I got my own office. It was newly mine, and remodeled and decorated to perfection as I knew it. I learned two weeks after I moved in that, yes, I was expected to clean the toilet. I actually laughed out loud when it struck me that here I am, a big-shot boss in his nice, fancy office, and . . . well, nobody else was going to do it.

Office management and building maintenance do not directly make money, but you have to do it. It would be ideal to spend two hours in the morning running the business and the other six hours of the day at the work that produces income. It isn't that easy. You need to divide your labor into doing the work and administering the business; and you need to pay close attention to when to administer and when to work. Otherwise, it is too easy to run amok trying to do everything at once haphazardly and not very well. Administrative tasks are essential to keep the business going, even if they don't add directly to the cash flow. The goal is to do them as efficiently as possible in order to leave uninterrupted time to do the work and cultivate new business.

On the other hand, thinking you have to do it all yourself is a trap. The ideal is to identify what you do well and to provide for someone else, even a part-time assistant, to do what you do less well. You will have to pay that person, but that is likely to cut into income less than trying to do everything yourself. It will also provide an element of quality that you can pass along to the client. It makes your services more valuable. We will take this up when I talk about organizing your work and hiring support staff.

When You Are Boss Clients Are Your Boss

As boss of the operation and master of all you survey, however, you are not entirely independent. You answer directly to the clients. Clients are more demanding than one boss. That is true whether you are a part-timer, a partner, or a sole practitioner. So be honest and ask yourself if you can deal directly with people personally and professionally, or if you are a shy number-cruncher who enjoys working in the back room. If you are the latter, you may want to hire someone to work with clients. Alone or as partners, you still must answer to the clients. Each of them cares only about his or her own issues and account. They don't give two hoots about your problems. If a client is upset with a tax return or if you made an error or omission, you will have a visitor. The classic example is when a client gets that ugly brown envelope from the Internal Revenue Service (IRS). It happens and it is going to happen. The item might even seem unimportant to you as a professional, and you will wonder why the client is bothering you with it. I guarantee it is a big deal to the client, and it is your responsibility to be able to deal with and solve it.

Why Leave a Big, Secure Company to Work on Your Own?

It is clear now that big companies are not as secure as they once had us all believe. With massive layoffs, mergers, down-sizing, restructuring, getting lean and mean—call it what you will—they dismiss professional and clerical people as readily as blue-collar workers. This book is almost certainly in the hands of more than a few people who were members of large corporate accounting departments and now find themselves relieved of their duties. My philosophy is that in a large company you are putting yourself at the mercy of others to look after you. Nobody can look after you better than you can.

Second, many people are locked in a position only for the security it seems to offer. They are in a golden cage. It may come with a very prestigious name and address but it is still a cage.

Third, for women the cage usually includes underpayment. That need not be permanent. The U.S. Bureau of Labor Statistics reported in 1991 that women were 51.2 percent of its "accountants and auditors" category. There are no numbers for women bookkeepers, but the American Society of Women Accountants, whose membership does not include bookkeepers, noted that the median income of self-employed women accountants, including certified public accountants (CPAs), was between $30,000 and $39,999 in 1992. While more of this self-employed group earned below $40,000, they also had the largest percentage (16.7) earning over $75,000. The Society reported that in 1992 17.2 percent of women accountants, including CPAs, were self-employed, up from 12.2 percent in 1977. Further, 28.2 percent of all women in accounting were owners of or partners in their own business. That's up from 4.9 percent in 1977! This is in line with other employment trends. According to recent surveys by the National Foundation for Women Business Owners and Dun & Bradstreet, women own 7.7 million businesses in the United States, about 30 percent of all U.S. businesses. These businesses employ 15.5 million people, approximately one-third more than Fortune 500 firms employ worldwide.

One last word: Alan S. Prahl, Executive Director of the National Association of Tax Practitioners (NATP), wrote us recently that the average NATP member is 52 years old. The prospect of so many tax preparers nearing retirement age could be a further enticement for younger bookkeeper/tax preparers.

Disadvantages Depend on You

Most business start-up books advise you to forget about having lots of free time. Baloney. I think it's a matter of personality. If you are a person who in a corporate setting works 12 hours a day and never takes vacations, you will probably be the same on your own. Likewise, if you don't want to push hard, then most likely you won't do it working for yourself. I personally don't believe you have to be a workaholic just to be successful. Forget about free time? Maybe.

The tax business is cyclical and that raises issues of budgeting time and money. The bulk of my revenue comes in the first quarter of the year. Then the next three quarters, especially the fourth, are thin. I *like* the cyclical nature of the business because I don't have to work hard for four or five months of the year. The downside is that it may not generate enough revenue and you have to fill out the rest of the year with bookkeeping or other services.

Another disadvantage is that the quarterly reports for all your bookkeeping clients and everybody else come due at the same time in April, a little before tax time. So you have to budget your clock and calendar to do both. That's where the long hours come in. They get longer because April is when everybody shows up who didn't come in March —or even February—when you asked them to. In this business we are the victims of other people's procrastination, as well as our own. That calls for a special mind set which I will touch on below.

Mental Requirements

I think the most important characteristic for running a business is confidence. It is the wellspring from which all other qualities flow. If you doubt yourself, you are going to feel insecure, especially when starting out. Consider yourself the authority. What other people say or do or think about you and your work is not important. By all means listen to your clients, but ignore the rest.

Next Four Pages:

The first Form 1040 in 1913 was four pages long, including one of instructions (see the next few pages). Individuals got a $3,000 deduction; married couples got $4,000. All of the 357,598 returns sent in were notarized, each was audited.

The tax started at one percent (1%); it was six percent (6%) on earnings above $500,000. Taxpayers' average income was $10,960, on which they paid an average tax of $78.

—SOI BULLETIN, Fall 1993, pp. 6-7.

TO BE FILLED IN BY COLLECTOR.

Form 1040.

INCOME TAX.

THE PENALTY
FOR FAILURE TO HAVE THIS RETURN IN THE HANDS OF THE COLLECTOR OF INTERNAL REVENUE ON OR BEFORE MARCH 1 IS $20 TO $1,000.
(SEE INSTRUCTIONS ON PAGE 4.)

TO BE FILLED IN BY INTERNAL REVENUE BUREAU.

List No. ....

.... District of ....

Date received ....

File No. ....

Assessment List ....

Page .... Line ....

UNITED STATES INTERNAL REVENUE.

RETURN OF ANNUAL NET INCOME OF INDIVIDUALS.
(As provided by Act of Congress, approved October 3, 1913.)

RETURN OF NET INCOME RECEIVED OR ACCRUED DURING THE YEAR ENDED DECEMBER 31, 191__
(FOR THE YEAR 1913, FROM MARCH 1, TO DECEMBER 31.)

Filed by (or for) .... of ....
                        (Full name of individual.)   (Street and No.)

in the City, Town, or Post Office of .... State of ....
                                    (Fill in pages 2 and 3 before making entries below.)

1. GROSS INCOME (see page 2, line 12) .... $ ....

2. GENERAL DEDUCTIONS (see page 3, line 7) .... $ ....

3. NET INCOME .... $ ....

Deductions and exemptions allowed in computing income subject to the normal tax of 1 per cent.

4. Dividends and net earnings received or accrued, of corporations, etc., subject to like tax. (See page 2, line 11) .... $ ....

5. Amount of income on which the normal tax has been deducted and withheld at the source. (See page 2, line 9, column A) ....

6. Specific exemption of $3,000 or $4,000, as the case may be. (See Instructions 3 and 19) ....

Total deductions and exemptions. (Items 4, 5, and 6) .... $ ....

7. TAXABLE INCOME on which the normal tax of 1 per cent is to be calculated. (See Instruction 3). $ ....

8. When the net income shown above on line 3 exceeds $20,000, the additional tax thereon must be calculated as per schedule below:

				INCOME.	TAX.
1 per cent on amount over $20,000 and not exceeding $50,000....				$	$ ....
2 " " 50,000 " " 75,000....					
3 " " 75,000 " " 100,000....					
4 " " 100,000 " " 250,000....					
5 " " 250,000 " " 500,000....					
6 " " 500,000					

Total additional or super tax .... $ ....

Total normal tax (1 per cent of amount entered on line 7).... $ ....

Total tax liability... $ ....

2

GROSS INCOME.

This statement must show in the proper spaces the entire amount of gains, profits, and income received by or accrued to the individual from all sources during the year specified on page 1.

DESCRIPTION OF INCOME.	A. Amount of income on which tax has been deducted and withheld at the source.				B. Amount of income on which tax has not been deducted and withheld at the source.			
1. Total amount derived from salaries, wages, or compensation for personal service of whatever kind and in whatever form paid.	$				$			
2. Total amount derived from professions, vocations, businesses, trade, commerce, or sales or dealings in property, whether real or personal, growing out of the ownership or use of or interest in real or personal property, including bonds, stocks, etc.								
3. Total amount derived from rents and from interest on notes, mortgages, and securities (other than reported on lines 5 and 6).								
4. Total amount of gains and profits derived from partnership business, whether the same be divided and distributed or not.								
5. Total amount of fixed and determinable annual gains, profits, and income derived from interest upon bonds and mortgages or deeds of trust, or other similar obligations of corporations, joint-stock companies or associations, and insurance companies, whether payable annually or at shorter or longer periods.								
6. Total amount of income derived from coupons, checks, or bills of exchange for or in payment of interest upon bonds issued in *foreign countries* and upon *foreign mortgages* or like obligations (not payable in the United States), and also from coupons, checks, or bills of exchange for or in payment of any dividends upon the stock or interest upon the obligations of foreign corporations, associations, and insurance companies engaged in business in foreign countries.								
7. Total amount of income received from fiduciaries.								
8. Total amount of income derived from any source whatever, not specified or entered elsewhere on this page.								
9. TOTALS.	$				$			
NOTE.—Enter total of Column A on line 5 of first page.								
10. AGGREGATE TOTALS OF COLUMNS A AND B					$			
11. Total amount of income derived from dividends on the stock or from the net earnings of corporations, joint-stock companies, associations, or insurance companies subject to like tax (To be entered on line 4 of first page.)					$			
12. TOTAL "Gross Income" (to be entered on line 1 of first page)					$			

3

GENERAL DEDUCTIONS.

1. The amount of necessary expenses actually paid in carrying on business, but not including business expenses of partnerships, and not including personal, living, or family expenses......	$		
2. All interest paid within the year on personal indebtedness of taxpayer.....................			
3. All national, State, county, school, and municipal taxes paid within the year (not including those assessed against local benefits)			
4. Losses actually sustained during the year incurred in trade or arising from fires, storms, or shipwreck, and not compensated for by insurance or otherwise			
5. Debts due which have been actually ascertained to be worthless and which have been charged off within the year..			
6. Amount representing a reasonable allowance for the exhaustion, wear, and tear of property arising out of its use or employment in the business, not to exceed, in the case of mines, 5 per cent of the gross value at the mine of the output for the year for which the computation is made, but no deduction shall be made for any amount of expense of restoring property or making good the exhaustion thereof, for which an allowance is or has been made..........			
7. Total "GENERAL DEDUCTIONS" (to be entered on line 2 of first page)			

AFFIDAVIT TO BE EXECUTED BY INDIVIDUAL MAKING HIS OWN RETURN.

I solemnly swear (or affirm) that the foregoing return, to the best of my knowledge and belief, contains a true and complete statement of all gains, profits, and income received by or accrued to me during the year for which the return is made, and that I am entitled to all the deductions and exemptions entered or claimed therein, under the Federal Income-tax Law of October 3, 1913.

Sworn to and subscribed before me this..........................

day of ...., 191

(Signature of individual.)

SEAL OF
OFFICER
TAKING
AFFIDAVIT.
....

....
(Official capacity.)

AFFIDAVIT TO BE EXECUTED BY DULY AUTHORIZED AGENT MAKING RETURN FOR INDIVIDUAL.

I solemnly swear (or affirm) that I have sufficient knowledge of the affairs and property of ....
to enable me to make a full and complete return thereof, and that the foregoing return, to the best of my knowledge and belief, contains a true and complete statement of all gains, profits, and income received by or accrued to said individual during the year for which the return is made, and that the said individual is entitled, under the Federal Income-tax Law of October 3, 1913, to all the deductions and exemptions entered or claimed therein.

Sworn to and subscribed before me this..........................

day of ...., 191

(Signature of agent.)

ADDRESS
IN FULL
....

....

SEAL OF
OFFICER
TAKING
AFFIDAVIT.
....

....
(Official capacity.)

c 2—7397   [SEE INSTRUCTIONS ON BACK OF THIS PAGE.]

4

INSTRUCTIONS.

1. This return shall be made by every citizen of the United States, whether residing at home or abroad, and by every person residing in the United States, though not a citizen thereof, having a *net income* of $3,000 or over for the taxable year, and *also* by every *nonresident alien* deriving income from property owned and business, trade, or profession carried on *in the United States* by him.

2. When an individual by reason of minority, sickness or other disability, or absence from the United States, is unable to make his own return, it may be made for him by his *duly authorized* representative.

3. The *normal tax* of 1 per cent shall be assessed on the total net income less the specific exemption of $3,000 or $4,000 as the case may be. (For the year 1913, the specific exemption allowable is $2,500 or $3,333.33, as the case may be.) If, however, the normal tax has been deducted and withheld on any part of the income at the source, or if any part of the income is received as dividends upon the stock or from the net earnings of any corporation, etc., which is taxable upon its net income, such income shall be deducted from the individual's total *net income* for the purpose of calculating the amount of income on which the individual is liable for the normal tax of 1 per cent by virtue of this return. (See page 1, line 7.)

4. The *additional or super tax* shall be calculated as stated on page 1.

5. This return shall be filed with the Collector of Internal Revenue for the district in which the individual resides if he has no other place of business, otherwise in the district in which he has his *principal place of business*; or in case the person resides in a foreign country, then with the collector for the district in which his principal business is carried on in the United States.

6. This return must be filed on or before the first day of March succeeding the close of the calendar year for which return is made.

7. The *penalty for failure to file the return within the time specified by law* is $20 to $1,000. In case of refusal or neglect to render the return within the required time (except in cases of sickness or absence), 50 per cent shall be added to amount of tax assessed. In case of false or fraudulent return, 100 per cent shall be added to such tax, and any person required by law to make, render, sign, or verify any return who makes any false or fraudulent return or statement with intent to defeat or evade the assessment required by this section to be made shall be guilty of a misdemeanor, and shall be fined not exceeding $2,000 or be imprisoned not exceeding one year, or both, at the discretion of the court, with the costs of prosecution.

8. When the return is not filed within the required time by reason of sickness or absence of the individual, an extension of time, not exceeding 30 days from March 1, within which to file such return, *may be granted* by the collector, *provided* an application therefor is made by the individual within the period for which such extension is desired.

9. This return properly filled out must be made under oath or affirmation. Affidavits may be made before any officer *authorized by law* to administer oaths. If before a justice of the peace or magistrate, not using a seal, a *certificate of the clerk of the court as to the authority* of such officer to administer oaths should be *attached to the return.*

10. Expense for medical attendance, store accounts, family supplies, wages of domestic servants, cost of board, room, or house rent for family or personal use, *are not expenses that can be deducted from gross income.* In case an individual owns his own residence he can not deduct the estimated value of his rent,

neither shall he be required to include such estimated rental of his home as income.

11. The farmer, in computing the net income from his farm for his annual return, shall include all moneys received for produce and animals sold, and for the wool and hides of animals slaughtered, provided such wool and hides are sold, and he shall deduct therefrom the sums actually paid as purchase money for the animals sold or slaughtered during the year.

When animals were raised by the owner and are sold or slaughtered he shall not deduct their value as expenses or loss. He may deduct the amount of money actually paid as expense for producing any farm products, live stock, etc. In deducting expenses for repairs on farm property the amount deducted must not exceed the amount actually expended for such repairs during the year for which the return is made. (See page 3, item 6.) The cost of replacing tools or machinery is a deductible expense to the extent that the cost of the new articles does not exceed the value of the old.

12. In calculating losses, only such losses as shall have been actually sustained and the amount of which has been definitely ascertained during the year covered by the return can be deducted.

13. Persons receiving fees or emoluments for professional or other services, as in the case of physicians or lawyers, should include all actual receipts for services rendered in the year for which return is made, together with all unpaid accounts, charges for services, or contingent income due for that year, if good and collectible.

14. Debts which were contracted during the year for which return is made, but found in said year to be worthless, may be deducted from gross income for said year, but such debts can not be regarded as worthless until after legal proceedings to recover the same have proved fruitless, or it clearly appears that the debtor is insolvent. If debts contracted prior to the year for which return is made were included as income in return for year in which said debts were contracted, and such debts shall subsequently prove to be worthless, they may be deducted under the head of losses in the return for the year in which such debts were charged off as worthless.

15. Amounts due or accrued to the individual members of a partnership from the net earnings of the partnership, whether apportioned and distributed or not, shall be included in the annual return of the individual.

16. United States pensions shall be included as income.

17. Estimated advance in value of real estate is not required to be reported as income, unless the increased value is taken up on the books of the individual as an increase of assets.

18. Costs of suits and other legal proceedings arising from ordinary business may be treated as an expense of such business, and may be deducted from gross income for the year in which such costs were paid.

19. An unmarried individual or a married individual not living with wife or husband shall be allowed an exemption of $3,000. When husband and wife live together they shall be allowed jointly a total exemption of only $4,000 on their aggregate income. They may make a joint return, both subscribing thereto, or if they have separate incomes, they may make separate returns; but in no case shall they jointly claim more than $4,000 exemption on their aggregate income.

20. In computing net income there shall be excluded the compensation of all officers and employees of a State or any political subdivision thereof, except when such compensation is paid by the United States Government.   c 1—7367

The second major character trait is flexibility. The nature of this business requires it, especially in tax practice. The law changes all the time. You must be able to ascertain your clients' needs and motivations then adapt them to the current tax code. Even clients who know very little about tax laws will come to you for the best deal they can get. If you can't meet their needs and motivations, you must be able to explain why meeting them is impossible or undesirable, and to make clear that you are on the clients' side and above all want to keep them from getting in trouble with the IRS.

You have to be flexible in your business practice. Clients' payment practices vary and need to be dealt with differently. You need to be flexible in scheduling—especially during tax season when, among everything else, those many clients show up a month late. You have to be willing to work nights, and to make appointments with clients on weekends and in the evening because they can't come in during the work day. You need flexibility, too, in your home life and in relations with your family.

Finally, you need a sense of authority. If you don't believe it, your clients won't. You must stand firm on ethical issues. It will create the atmosphere for the rest of your career. If a client wants something illegal or unethical you have to stand your ground. You can be wishy-washy on collecting the fee and on the delivery of some services, but you cannot be wishy-washy if it would compromise you ethically or legally. It goes without saying, but I will say it anyway, that trustworthiness and honesty are at the heart of this business.

What You Need to Know

To succeed at bookkeeping and tax preparation you need some technical knowledge of bookkeeping, double entry, single entry, or both, and you need to have taken a course on the Tax Code. Let's say you are a bookkeeper in a small firm or in the accounting department of a large company. You like the work and you are good at it. But perhaps you don't like your situation, you are facing a layoff, or you just want to spread your wings. To engineer a smooth transition into self-employment, begin to educate yourself. Courses are available at community colleges or adult schools. H&R Block runs an excellent and current program of tax courses. To find when and where H&R Block is giving its next course, telephone the company's local branch and ask for information. Also, you can start part time as I did and learn in easy bites from an established practitioner.

If you lack the basic skills and setting up a practice is a long-range goal, you might read the classified ads in your newspaper for an entry-level position to learn on the job. Meanwhile take all the courses you can. If there is no adult-education program or community college in your area, see if your state college system has an extension or correspondence program. Your public library will help you find them.

If I had it to do over again I would spend more time working with somebody else and learning the business. A lot of my floundering around at the beginning was from not learning from somebody else's mistakes. Most owners of bookkeeping firms recommend two or three years' prior experience with an active firm, or in a retail or industrial company's bookkeeping department, as long as the department has high standards of practice. If you don't work for the niftiest bookkeeping department in the world, you can extend your skills by doing bookkeeping on the side and supplementing your experience with community college or adult school courses. An added advantage of this in-house approach is that, in a large city, bookkeeping experience in a certain kind of industry like laundries, restaurants, drugstores, contractors, and so on, could allow you to specialize. Specialization can lead to real efficiencies, economies, and sometimes more money.

Business? It's quite simple. It's other people's money.

—Alexandre Dumas, fils (1824-1895)
The Question of Money (1857, Act II, Sc. 7.)

To find somebody to work for and learn from, use the Yellow Pages and canvass established professionals in your area like CPAs, public accountants, tax preparers, and enrolled agents. The time to pursue this employment is not in January when the tax business starts up, but in October. Don't bother with anyone who would hire in January during the tax season. Any tax preparation office worth the name will have a staff of veterans already working for them.

Check your state's laws and regulations. All states have laws that regulate certain levels of public accounting and the use of certain titles. Requirements differ from state to state and all change continually. The

Appendix gives a list of relevant agencies in each state; in most states the agency is called a Board of Accountancy or the like.

Honing Your Skills

If you are already in the business, you have an advantage by being plugged into the professional societies and the continuing education requirements needed to increase your skills and pursue licensure or professional designations. It is very important to cultivate a group of colleagues to whom you can turn. In rural and small-town areas colleagues are usually very helpful and liberal with their expenditure of time and knowledge to help out. It is all right for a beginner to call on or make inquiries of established practitioners. Even in urban areas it is worth doing, but it takes judgment. Some practitioners may be cranky and will refuse to talk, but usually the next one will be very helpful. Be congenial and try to return the favor as best you can when the time comes.

Another possible advantage of being out on your own is having access to others who know more about a particular subject than you do. A cadre of colleagues or group of friends who specialize in different areas is very valuable. When you work for a large office or firm and don't know the answer, you can always go down the hall to the person who does. Out on your own, that person is not down the hall but in another firm that may also be a competitor and charging $100 an hour to answer the questions you want to ask. So it is necessary to cultivate colleagues.

While you are at it, don't hesitate to contact other professionals —insurers, lawyers, engineers, and the like—when you need their specialized knowledge. As part of your networking campaign it can help build better recognition in the community and provide sources of potential referrals.

You need to understand your limits, that is, what services you can provide in a timely manner and which are simply beyond your capacity for lack of knowledge or staff. If you don't have 15 auditors you don't take the school district as a client, but you might take on the superintendent of schools as an individual client. Big staffs take big jobs, small operators take small ones. A great way to get experience is to work for a large firm that needs a part-time bookkeeper. Look for an existing active bookkeeping or accounting practice. A larger firm gearing up to push into tax preparation or a big job can provide an opportunity to do a task otherwise beyond your capabilities and at the same time to learn from it.

For example, I have one full-time employee, but during tax time two or three bookkeepers work with me by contract. I am the kind of guy you would want to look for to learn how the bookkeeping business works. Convince me that you are good, and I'll hire you and you will learn from me.

Plan Ahead and You're on Your Way

After you get what you can use from these pages, and as part of choosing your market and setting up, write out at least a minimal business plan. It doesn't matter at first how informal the plan is, but it should address the essential questions *in writing*. (No keeping them all in your head where they get lost, change to suit your mood, and never exactly mesh.) We won't discuss business plans until the end of this book, after I have told you everything I think you should consider for a complete and realistic plan.

That's it for starters. You need adequate training in bookkeeping and at least two years' experience in a small firm. You need management ability or at least an idea of what it is. You need to be willing to take risks. In some states you may need to be registered and licensed. You will also need money to get started and keep the doors open for the next six months or year. Finally, you need a plan. Don't worry. You already have most of what you need. We will deal with the rest.

*While often you will need to
rely on information provided
by professionals, you must
feel confident that you understand the general rules and
know whom to turn to when a
problem arises.*

Technicalities and Taxes

STARTING a business—any business—is a little like creating a whole new person. You have to name it, register it for taxes, find it a place to live, insure it, and perhaps enter its name on the public records. As a commercial enterprise it can get into, and be the victim of, as much mischief as any real person; so you need to consider a few legal, tax, and insurance matters.

Naming the Business

I don't think that a catchy business name or phrase is necessary or desirable for a bookkeeping and tax-preparation service. Your clients are there to find out if you know your business; so you might as well use your own name. If you use a name other than your own—for example, to identify your services as a specialized practice—banks will require you to establish a DBA (doing business as) and provide the necessary licenses before opening an account. This is not a problem if you use your own name or a variation of it. A fictitious business name (the DBA) in California includes one that does not use the owner's surname or suggests additional owners, as in "& Associates"or "& Company."

If you have a reason to use a fictitious or assumed business name, you must record it and comply with the other legal requirements. In

California that means filing a Fictitious Name Statement with the County Clerk, at $25 per named individual, and publishing the statement in a newspaper of general circulation. Here if you use a fictitious business name but do not record it, the business cannot sue in its own name. Recording the name also lets anyone else know that using it might infringe on an active trade name. It also tells who owns the business in case— heaven forbid—someone decides to sue you and the business. Fictitious business names have to be renewed periodically. In California that's every five years. The laws in your state are probably different.

If you use one, pick a fictitious business name that no one else is using, that describes your business, and that is easy to remember and say. Pick a name you can grow into. If you sell the business, the buyer would be buying name recognition. As I say, my preference as a professional is to use my own name. One reason to use a fictitious name may be, however, to distinguish the nature of specialized services in a large metropolitan market. For example, you would have ample reason to name your business "Truckers' Bookkeeping Service," "Medical Business Services" or "Restaurant Financial Systems" if you restricted its practice to haulers, health-care providers, or food-service entities.

Whether or not you use a fictitious business name, you will have to take out a local business license. These are regulatory and revenue generating devices; you needn't take an exam or qualify for one. The local government will want to be sure that you comply with all local ordinances, including building, zoning, and property tax laws. Proof of compliance with some of these may require a permit, variance, or waiver. Check with your local authorities and comply as necessary. Starting out on the right foot here can prevent more expensive trouble later on.

Form of Business

There isn't much choice for the form of the business. Unless you contemplate beginning with someone else, the business will start as a sole proprietorship. If you start as a partnership, you want a written partnership agreement that clearly describes each partner's responsibilities and the division of duties.

Consider a partnership only if you know that the other person's personality, skills, and goals complement and are compatible with your own. Agree in advance on who will do what. Put everything in the written agreement. Provide for the partnership's dissolution by death, disability, or incompatibility by executing a partnership buy-sell agreement. It should state how to appraise the partnership's value and how the remaining partner will pay for it. A buy-out usually requires financing or carry-back financing. Have a good small-business lawyer prepare the agreement, or use a partnership book to draft your own and have that lawyer review the agreement. A good introduction to partnership problems and agreements is *The Partnership Book*, by Denis Clifford and Ralph Warner, published by Nolo Press.

It makes no sense to start out as a corporation because there is no protection or corporate veil for service-providing professionals like lawyers, accountants, or tax preparers. And there are additional costs that make incorporation hard to justify, unless the business moves up to the big money and can enjoy corporate tax advantages.

The Legal Proprieties

Legal paperwork is minimal in this business. Certified public accountants use an engagement letter. It lays out what services they provide, what their responsibilities are to the client, what the client's responsibilities are to them, and that the client agrees to those principles. For a new bookkeeper and tax preparer that may be a little pretentious. I have found that as I went along I learned which clients I could trust and which I could not. My policy is to keep clear of the ones I can't trust and keep the ones I can. It works the other way, too; if they don't like me, they go away. I don't think contracts are necessary. That's a personal opinion. You might want to talk to a lawyer about it, but I'll bet I can predict what the lawyer will say.

Building the business on trust works on another front. If you are fortunate enough to be in a rural or small-town area like me, you can build personal relationships with people in the local offices of the IRS and the state and local taxing authorities. It doesn't hurt to build a good relationship with auditors and line staff. As part of building a good relationship, the one thing you want to do is to handle all government inquiries promptly and professionally. First, the client will be very nervous about the inquiry, and by all means you want to reassure the client and have the inquiry conducted in an atmosphere of mutual trust and respect. Second, your good relations will help smooth things for you and your client on into the future. The key is to handle all interaction with the IRS and local taxing authorities ethically and expeditiously.

A final legal consideration is selecting a lawyer for the business. In its formative stages you may want to find a lawyer who specializes in small-business contracts and other agreements. You need to rely on word of mouth and the experiences of friends and colleagues. Yellow Page advertisements are not very useful, although they may be the only way to get a list of lawyer's names to run by other people in business. If you can't get other people's opinions, ask the lawyers to give you clients' names as references.

The British Parliament has no right to tax the Americans. . . . Taxation and representation are inseparably united. God hath joined them; no British Parliament can put them asunder. To endeavor to do so is to stab at our very vitals.

—Charles Pratt, Earl Camden (1714-1794),
Speech to the House of Lords, 1765

Taxation without representation is tyranny.

—Watchword of the American Revolution.

Employees and the Law

An employee's employment and insurance rights are complicated and detailed. All of Chapter 11 considers aspects of hiring and using employees. If you plan to move up to being an employer, you should consult someone, perhaps a good attorney, to help you understand what the employee's rights are. It is important to do this ahead of time and incorporate it into some sort of employment manual, job description, or policy statement in order to preclude potential conflicts. The time to start learning about employee rights and laws is before you have become an employer and have a problem on your hands.

Before consulting a lawyer about employment problems, I recommend reading Fred S. Steingold's *Legal Guide for Starting and Running a Small Business*, published by Nolo Press. You will notice that I keep referring to this publisher's books. They are written in plain English by lawyers for non-lawyers and on the whole are reasonably reliable. They will at least save you money by helping to organize your questions if you seek legal help.

Your local Chamber of Commerce is an additional resource to investigate early on. California's has an excellent catalog of reasonably priced booklets and pamphlets that deal with employee matters. Those in other states may provide similar services. Joining the local Chamber is not a bad idea, anyway, as a way to get involved in your business community and to take advantage of the assistance the Chamber offers.

Insurance

You will need to insure the business against risks that as an individual you may never encounter or even contemplate. First, you may have to insure yourself as the sole source of your own and your family's income. Statistics show that the probability of becoming incapacitated and unable to continue in your profession is seven times greater in almost any age group than the possibility of dying. If you suffer some disabling condition as a result of an accident you will find it extremely difficult to make a living. If your profession is your only income and you don't have someone or something to fall back on, then disability insurance is critical. When you get banged up and can't carry on the business, you don't produce any revenue and quickly go broke. Add to

For better or worse the Boston Tea Party still characterizes many Americans' attitude toward taxes. (Print by Currier & Ives.)

it the cost of being sick, and the incentive for coverage becomes all the greater.

While there isn't a whole lot of risk of getting hurt directly in the tax-preparation and bookkeeping business, the world is full of dangers. If you are an active person who spends weekends mountain climbing or motorcycle racing you have a higher than average probability of suffering some debilitating injury. Even if you lead what you consider a quiet life, your home is not free of danger, and you probably spend as much time as any other American in an automobile, a condition of real and calculable risk.

Whether you are renting your office facilities or operating out of your home, or if you own or are in the process of buying your own office building, you definitely want comprehensive coverage against fire, theft, and vandalism as it affects your business and its assets. If operating out of your home, check with your insurance agent to ensure that your business activities do not compromise your homeowner's insurance and, in fact, that your homeowner's insurance and whatever extended coverage you have will take care of you and not be jeopardized by your business activities. It is hard to imagine how bookkeeping and tax preparation will cause such problems, but it's worth checking out.

You will need the standard business coverage, like premises, loss, and liability insurance. If you are certified for tax preparation or accounting, there are firms that will provide insurance that covers you in the event of a lawsuit resulting from an oversight. Liability coverage for tax practitioners and bookkeepers falls under what is called "Errors and Omissions" insurance. It is to protect you in case you made a mistake in conducting the client's business. The important thing is that a lawsuit may have nothing to do with any oversight by you or your company, but everything to do with a client's perception of an oversight. I have been fortunate in this, but clients have been known to sue and ask questions later. Errors and omissions insurance can prevent your losing everything you own if an arbitration or court proceeding goes against you. You can also extend coverage to employees if you provide the carrier with their qualifications. Be very sure you know what the insurance covers and when it took effect.

I might interject at this point that, if you prepare taxes, you want to be sure to write notes to each client's file of agreed upon decisions about gray areas in interpretation of the law. Because, if the client is audited, the auditor will ask your client why he or she did this or that. Your client will say, "My tax person told me to." You don't want to be in that position. Educate the client and have the client make the decision as far as possible. Then document it and keep it available. It's a lot of work but can be invaluable if there is a disagreement later on.

Umbrella policies for coverage in excess of other plans can usually be acquired in increments of a million dollars for a very reasonable additional charge. As your profile rises along with your popularity in the community, the likelihood becomes greater that you will become the target of some legitimate or illegitimate claim. So, the nominal sum necessary to carry an umbrella policy could be well worth the money.

You might also want to inquire about: valuable papers insurance to protect against the loss of client records and important practice documents; business interruption insurance to guarantee an income if your building or professional equipment is damaged; overhead insurance to cover fixed expenses, including salaries, rent, and utilities should you be incapacitated for a long time.

If you have employees, state law will mandate that you carry workers' compensation insurance. A sole practitioner need not—indeed cannot—carry it on himself or herself. It covers employees for work-related injuries. It may be hard to imagine a work-related injury in an office setting, but the risks are surprising. For example a file cabinet or drawer can fall on someone's foot. Someone can strain a back moving furniture or lifting a box of copy paper. There is no choice; you have got to have the darn stuff, and it serves a useful function. Payment for workers' compensation coverage is based on total payroll expenses and the kinds of work performed. Clerical duties are among the lowest risk category and, therefore, carry the lowest mandatory premium for coverage. You may want to carry some liability insurance in case the employee slips and falls on your floor. Although it is not specifically related to the kind of business you engage in, it is a general insurance risk and must be covered. Finally, ask about non-owner automobile insurance to cover an employee's car accident while on the job.

If you are not well versed in the details of insurance and retirement coverage you should seek the help of an expert, but be keenly aware of the difference between an expert and a salesperson. There is a swarm of salespeople with all kinds of pre-packaged retirement plans and pre-packaged insurance products that *they* are absolutely certain will meet your needs. It is you, however, who must ultimately be responsible for making the decision, and you will do better to consult someone whose advice is fee-based rather than paid from a commission on their sales. It will at least give you a better feeling of getting an unbiased analysis of your needs.

Almost all the things covered in this chapter compel you to rely on information provided by professionals, but it is your responsibility to seek out this information and gain a comfort level about it within your own experience. You must feel confident that you understand the general rules, and that you know to whom to turn and where to go if a problem arises.

Taxes

My views on the business's taxes will be brief because if you are not already very familiar with the subject, you probably soon will be. Document your business activities, keep track of income and expenses, and remember the taxing authorities are more concerned that you report all your income than in what deductions and expenses offset it. You can get in an awful lot more trouble for under-reporting income than for over-reporting expenses.

The best way to calculate all your expenses is to set up a spreadsheet of start-up needs and their costs. Then increase your costliest estimate by 50 percent.

3

Finances and Start-Up Costs

ONE attraction of this business is that start-up takes a relatively low capital outlay. The main tool of the trade is a computer system. The cheapest approach to start-up, of course, is to begin part time in your home, without necessarily abandoning your primary job or major employment. If you are at the point of wanting to jump in with both feet, however, then you need to step back and analyze several things.

Finances

First, how much money do you have in the bank? There should be enough to cover not only start-up costs, but to carry you until you break even and reach profitability. After your savings, the likeliest sources of money are family and friends. This has real disadvantages, especially if worse comes to worst and you can't pay the money back. Money problems have probably broken up more families and friendships than anything else. If you do borrow from friends or relatives, draft a formal loan agreement and follow it.

While a commercial loan is safely impersonal, it would be very unusual for a bank or commercial lending institution to help a small-business person just starting out unless the loan was secured with an additional asset. If you don't object to encumbering an asset, consider a loan against your life insurance policy or a home equity loan. It may be worth contacting the Small Business Administration (SBA). It has numerous programs available, but its funds are often hard to tap. The SBA licenses independent small-business investment companies (SBICs) to lend to small-business people. The local SBA can provide a list of them in your area. If nothing else, the SBA is a good source of information on managing a small business.

Opening a small business on borrowed capital usually depends on immediate needs and how easily you think you can pay back the loan. For instance, if your start-up involves purchasing a going concern, there may already be the prospect of enough income to cover loan payments. In any case, if your perception of income, expense, and time to break-even suggest that added capital will help get you started, contact some commercial lenders and work through their loan applications. These in themselves can be an education and a deciding factor. If you need a cosigner on a loan, be careful. The cosigner's potential liability is greater than yours in case you default. Even if you discharged the debt through a Chapter 7 bankruptcy, the cosigner would still be liable. A cosigner can be protected through a Chapter 13 bankruptcy, in which debts are paid off through future income.

Alternatively, if you need extra capital but can't or won't borrow the money, you might investigate equity rather than debt financing, that is to say, find a silent or limited partner to be paid off from the proceeds

---

Facing Page:

No one is certain how double-entry bookkeeping originated, but its first formal exposition appeared in 1494 in Fra Luca Pacioli's SUMMA DE ARITHMETICA. . . . Pacioli took orders late in life, primarily for safe travel during that turbulent era in Italian history. A mathematician, scholar, writer, lecturer, first occupant of the chair of mathematics at Milan, and associate of Leonardo da Vinci, Pacioli has probably had a far greater effect on people's daily lives than his more famous contemporary.

Diftinctio nona. Tractatus .xi°. De fcripturis

Commo fe debiano faldare tutte le partite del quaderno vechio:e i chi:e per che e de la fu
ma fumarum del dare e delauere ultimo fcontro del bilancio.   ca°.:4
Del modo e ordi a faper tenere le fcripture menute cōmo fono fcripti de manolfe familia
ri policçe:pcefſi:fentēnc e altri iftrumēti e del registro de le lettere ipo:tāti.   ca°.:5
Epilogo o uero fūmaria recolta de tutto el pzefente tractato:acio con bzeue fubftātia fe ha
bia mandare a memozia le cofe dette.   ca°.:6

Diftinctio.nona.Tractatus.xi°.pticularis de cōputis z fcripturis.

De quelle cofe che fono neceffarie al uero mercatante:e de lozdine a fape bē tenere vn q̄/
derno cō fuo gioznale i vinegia e anche p ognialtro luogo.   Capitolo primo.

Y reuerenti fubditi de.U.D.S.Magnanimo.D. acio a pieno
de tutto lozdine mercantefco habino el bifogno:deliberai.(olt°.
le cofe dinançe i q̄ſta nra opa ditte) ancoza particular tractato
grandemēte neceſſario cōpillare.E in q̄ſto folo lo ifcerto: p che
a ogniloro occurrēça el pfente libzo li poſſa feruire. Si del mo /
do a conti e fcripture:cōmo de ragioni.E per eſſo intendo dar/
li nozma fufficiente e baftante in tenere ordinatamente tutti lor
conti e libzi. Pero che. (cōmo ſi ſā)tre cofe maxime fono opoz
tunc:a chi uole con debita diligētia mercantare.De le q̄ilapozi
ſima e la pecunia numerata e ogni altra faculta fu:ftantiale. Ju
xta illud pl°y vnū aliquid neceffariozū e fubstantia.Sēça el cui
fuffragio mal ſi po el.manegio traficante exercitare. Buēga che
molti gia nudi cō bona fede cōmençando:de grā faccde habio fatto.E mediante lo credito
fedelmēte feruato i magne richeçce ſiēno peruenuti.Che aſai p ytalia difcurrēdo nabiamo
cognofciuti. E piu gia nele grā republiche non ſi poteua dire:che la fede del bon mercatan
te.E a quella ſi fermaua loz giuramento:dicēdo. A la fe de real mercatante.E cio nō deuel
fcre admirarione:cōcioſia che i la fede catolicamēte ognuno ſi faluer:e fença lci ſia ipoſſibile
piacere a dio. La fecōda cofa che ſi recerca al debito trafico:ſie che ſia buon ragionēri:e
pmpto cōputiſta.E p queſto cōfequire.(difopza cōmo fe ueduto)dal pzicipio alafine: ha
uemo iducto regole e canoni a ciafcuna opatione requiſiti.Jn modo che da ſe:ogni diligē
te lectoze.tutto potra ipzendere.E chi di questa pte non foſſe bene armato:la fequēte in ua
no li ferebbe.   La.3°.e vltima cofa opoztuna ſie:che cō bello ozdie tutte fue faccde debita
mēte difponga:acio con bzeuita:poſſa de ciafcūa hauer noritia:quanto aloz debito e anche
credito:che circa altro non fatēde el trafico.E q̄ſta pte fra laltre e alozo utiliſſim a:che i lor
faccde altramēte regerfi:feria ipoſſibile:fēça debito ordine de fcripture.E fēça alcū repoſo la
loz mēte fempze ſtaria in gran trauagli.E po acio con laltre q̄ſta poſſino hauere.el pfēte tra
ctato ozdiai.Del q̄le fe da el mō a tutte fozti de fcripture:a ca°.p ca°.pcedēdo.E bē che nō
ſi poſſa gufi apōto tutto el bifogno fcriuere.Nō dimeno p q̄l che fe dira.El pegrino ingeḡa
glūcal.vo laplicara.   E feruaremo i eſſo el mō de vinegia:q̄le certamēte fra glialtri e molto
da cōmēdare.E mediante q̄illo i ogni altro fe pozra guidare.E q̄ſto dinidirēmo i.2.pti pri
cipali. Luna chiamaremo iuētario.E laltra difpōe.E p°.de luna:e poi de laltra fucceſſiua
mēte fe dira fcōdo lozdie:i.per la q̄l facilmēte el lectoze pozra le
occur.zētie trouare fecondo el numero de fuoi capitoli e carti.

Di cō lo debito ozdie che faſpecta uol fap bē tenere vn q̄derno cō lo fuo giozna
le a q̄l che qui fe dira con diligētia ſtia a tēto.E acio.bē fintēda el pceſſo idurre/
mo i cāpo vno che mo dinouo cōmēçi a traficare cōmo p ozdie deba procedere
neltenere foi conti e fcripture:aciochc fucitamēte ogni cofa poſſi ritrouare poſta
al fuo luogo p che nō afcetrandole cofe debitamēte a li fuoi luoghi ucrebbe i grandiſſimi tra
uagli e cōfuſiōi de tutte fue faccde.Jurta cōe dictū vbi nō e ozdo ibi eſt cōtuſio.E pero a p
fecto documēto dogni mercatante de tutto nro pceſſo f aremo cōmo di fopza e ditto.:.pti
pncipali. Lcq̄li aptamēte q̄ fequēte chiariremo:acio fructo falutifero fabia ipzēdere.E p:ia
dimoftrando ch cofa ſia iuētario e cōmo fabia fare De la p°pte pncipale de q̄ſto tractato
detra iuētario.E che cofa ſia iuētario:e cōme fra mercatanti fabia fare. ca°.2   Cōuiene
adonca p°mēte pfupponere e imaginare che ogni opante e moſſo dalfine.E p poter q̄llo
debitamēte cōfeq̄re fa o zni fuo ſfozço nel fuo pceſſo.vnde el fine de q̄lūche traficante e de
cōfequire licito e cōpetēte guadagno p fua fubſtētariōe .E po fempze con lo nome de nro
domcnedio:debiano cōmençare lozo faccnde.Ei nel pu°. dognt loz fcripture:el fuo fanctc

The first page of section IX of Pacioli's Summa, which includes his discussion of double-entry bookkeeping.

of the business. Obviously this can be complicated and needs professional assistance to set up. A final source of added financing would be a second income, preferably your spouse's or "significant other's." This second-income approach would impose an intolerable burden if it were your income, and you tried to start up with too many hours a week.

I avoided, or at least mitigated, the financing issue by starting slow while doing something else and letting the business pay for itself as it went along. Besides keeping costs down, this method provides an opportunity to feel out the business and see whether it suits your temperament. My own start-up proceeded very slowly and very inexpensively. Instead of going right out and acquiring a computer and software, and spending a lot of money, I used a processing service where I paid a fee and filled out worksheets with the clients' information, and the service processed the information with *its* computer and software. The final product was all nicely printed up and sent back in a ready-to-go package to turn over to the client.

This is still an attractive alternative to investing heavily in the most powerful computer you can get, a laser printer, fax-modem, CD-ROM drive and disks, and what have you. If you decide to start out part time and use an outside tax processing service as I did, then start-up cost could be very low. I know of one service that required only a $300 first-time deposit. For established customers the deposit dropped to about $100 or so. They provided the forms you needed in order to start processing returns through the service. If you performed according to the contract you got the deposit back or had it credited to you in some other form. You can find these services in professional publications, which are available at your local public library. Nowadays batch service bureaus also offer standardized programming packages; some have free pick up and delivery; one I will discuss later has gone on-line in a big way.

The Full-Time Start-Up

If you decide to open an office full time, you will need a shopping list. Get on the telephone and check with city hall. Call real estate agents, furniture stores, office supply outlets, and insurance companies. Work out what your real costs will be. A sample spreadsheet appears in the Appendix.

First, prioritize your expenditures. Unless you came into a pot of money and can't wait to spend it all, you are not going to purchase all of your furnishings, equipment, and supplies right away. Some things, like a computer and software, are essential and take precedence over the oriental carpet in the waiting room. Business cards and enough telephone lines are more important than an executive swivel chair. Your gradual acquisition of office equipment should mesh with the business's growth and development. Keying your purchases to a business plan can keep expenditures under control and consistent with your level of business activity.

. . . There are three things needed by any one who wishes to carry on business carefully. The most important of these is cash or any equivalent. . . . The second thing . . . is to be a good bookkeeper and ready mathematician. . . . The third and last thing is to arrange all the transactions in such a systematic way that one may understand each one of them at a glance.

—Fra Luca Pacioli (1445?-1509)
SUMMA DE ARITHMETICA, 1494

Most of us are highly susceptible to painting a rosy picture of any new direction we decide to take, and it is human nature to believe everything is going to go the way we want. My advice is to draft that business plan, even a minimal one, and think out the cost analysis carefully. The best way to calculate all your expenses is to set up a simple spreadsheet of start-up needs and their costs. Then increase your most costly estimate by 50 percent. That way you may approach reality. Analyze your living expenses. If you are starting cold turkey in this business, be sure you have the wherewithal to sustain yourself for a year and be ready to tough it out without making any profits. Before committing yourself to any hard work get your numbers down on paper so you have a map of your campaign.

In addition to covering set-up expenses and operating expenses to break-even, initial cash reserves should include a contingency reserve for emergencies (and opportunities). Remember to include opening or pre-opening expenses like rental advances and security deposits, space renovation and decoration, telephone installation costs, utility deposits, insurance, signage and any exterior work, and freight charges. Operating expense forecasts should include fixed costs like rent, utilities, telephone, advertising and promotion, insurance, janitorial services, security, trash pick-up, perhaps loan repayment, updates for tax preparation software and other professional information services, any professional subscriptions and dues, and miscellaneous. Variable expenses may include the costs of batch processing services for returns, copying, temporary help, legal and other professional services, supplies, and miscellaneous again. Now that I have cudgeled you with this stream of expenses we can consider how to trim and manage them.

Furnishings and Equipment

The major expense these days is a computer. It is such an important item it takes up the entire next chapter. In addition to a computer, however, you will need desks, chairs, file cabinets, lamps, and other furnishings and equipment. Buy good quality but used. It doesn't make sense to pay for new items that depreciate enormously as soon as they leave the warehouse. It's like buying a brand new automobile. It smells newest and best just as it rolls off the lot and drops 25 percent of its value in the gutter. Let someone else take the hit while you pay 35 cents on the dollar.

Often it is worth travelling a hundred miles to the nearest big city and renting a truck to haul the goods home.

Ads like this for cheap but high-quality and attractive used office furniture are common in big-city newspapers.

In some large urban areas there are established markets for used office furniture and stores that specialize in it. They buy liquidated office furniture in bulk. Consulting firms, lending institutions, and glitzy professional groups merge, close branches, go bankrupt, or even remodel and get rid of perfectly good but slightly dated office furniture. If you read big city telephone directories and classified ads you will find the stores that specialize in this kind of merchandise. They buy cheap and usually pass the savings to their customers. Check them out to familiarize yourself with the stock. You may have to wait a few weeks for a major liquidation to replenish it; so wait. Often it is worth travelling a hundred miles to the nearest big city and renting a truck to haul the goods home. Used equipment does not have so well-developed a market, but often dealers in new equipment take good used machinery as trade-ins. They might even service them and issue limited warranties.

Design Costs

Bookkeeping and tax preparation is not a business where eye-catching logos are going to build up the business any more than a catchy business name. You should, however, have business cards and stationery designed to look pleasing and professional. Usually a good printer has a portfolio of designs for you to choose from. The cost for these services is usually included in the price of printing. Again, don't purchase more than you will use up in the first six months' or year's trial run. Even once established, be wary of over-purchasing supplies and equipment, including business cards and stationery. More on this later.

Telephones and Faxes

You will need at least two telephone lines, and perhaps three if you use a fax or fax-modem. Operating out of your home, which I will discuss later, you can have your telephone company install a second residential line and convert one line to business purposes. This can be cheaper than getting commercial service. Check with your local carrier to see what the company's policies are. In fact, with the continuing deregulation of the industry, you may want to contact your inside installer first to help shop for the best combination of local and long-distance communications services.

It is best to have a separate line for fax and modem. You should have at least two voice lines, anyway, to handle people who telephone while you are on the line. A telephone with a call-waiting feature may be a cheaper alternative, but many callers don't like the clicking while they are talking to you. If you can't afford three lines shop around for a fax-modem that can tell a voice, from a fax or data call, and switch to the

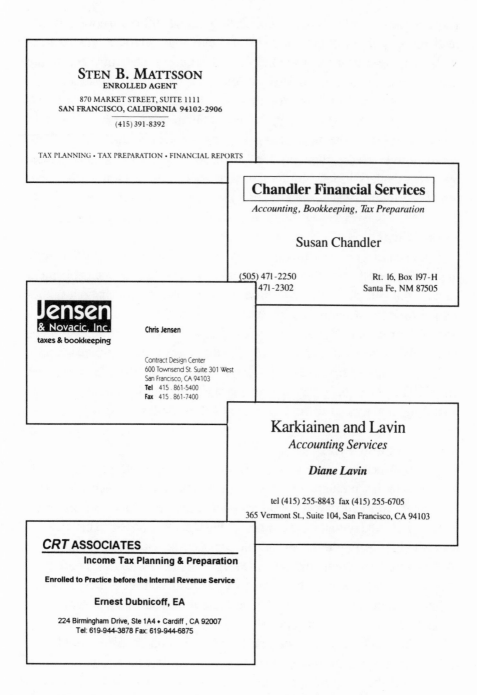

STEN B. MATTSSON
ENROLLED AGENT

870 MARKET STREET, SUITE 1111
SAN FRANCISCO, CALIFORNIA 94102-2906

(415) 391-8392

TAX PLANNING · TAX PREPARATION · FINANCIAL REPORTS

Chandler Financial Services

Accounting, Bookkeeping, Tax Preparation

Susan Chandler

(505) 471-2250   Rt. 16, Box 197-H
471-2302   Santa Fe, NM 87505

**Jensen
& Novacic, Inc.**
taxes & bookkeeping

Chris Jensen

Contract Design Center
600 Townsend St. Suite 301 West
San Francisco, CA 94103
Tel 415 . 861-5400
Fax 415 . 861-7400

Karkiainen and Lavin
Accounting Services

Diane Lavin

tel (415) 255-8843 fax (415) 255-6705
365 Vermont St., Suite 104, San Francisco, CA 94103

CRT ASSOCIATES
Income Tax Planning & Preparation

Enrolled to Practice before the Internal Revenue Service

Ernest Dubnicoff, EA

224 Birmingham Drive, Ste 1A4 • Cardiff , CA 92007
Tel: 619-944-3878 Fax: 619-944-6875

A sampling of business cards, any of which a good printer can run up. Two are for practitioners qualified to offer accounting services, but all state qualifications clearly and with a minimum of fuss.

proper channel. Currently all competitive modems offer those features. Some even have built-in voice mail and cue your callers to leave a message then record it. A few will contact a pager. Answering services seem to have all but disappeared with the advance of increasingly flexible answering devices. A word of warning—this is not a joke—don't get an answering machine with voice mail that comes across as smarter than your clients. They won't like it, especially when the machine cuts them off after leading them through half a dozen touch-tone options, as some have done to me on occasion.

You may even have a choice other than the above paraphernalia. Our local Bell system offers a full-featured answering service for about $20 per month that may outdo call-waiting and answering machines. It also supplements them. The system's standard recorded service takes your calls after certain number of rings or if your line is busy. You can leave personal greetings up to two minutes long and the service will take up to 30 three-minute messages over a 14-day period. It can take multiple calls, simultaneously if necessary. It can also page you, and you can restrict paging to urgent messages. It features a transfer to voice mail that eventually takes the caller to a live person. And you can control all of this remotely with touch-tone commands. Your local Bell's business marketing unit should be able to explain what is available in your area.

Copiers

I have been in business and doing very well at the same location for six years. I do not own a photocopy machine and, all things being equal, don't anticipate getting one anytime soon. The only copiers worth owning cost as much as a small automobile. They cost as much to service, too. Personal copiers won't stand up to business use, and cheap business copiers are well named. It doesn't make sense to buy a copier if you can use the nearest copy shop. Once or twice daily I have our accumulation copied around the corner on the best machine in town for very little money. As a regular customer I am billed monthly and get a discount after 250 copies. I think the supposed convenience of having your own copier is overshadowed by the headaches and doubtful quality of a cheap machine.

A qualification: I am within a block of that best copy service in town. My assistant informs me that if I move to a bigger office three or four blocks away, we need to get an office copier. Fine, I will get a cheap one for the occasional snapshot but save our big, important jobs for the copy service. Multiple runs from my laser printer substitute for "copies" of tax returns. Unless I need to copy a signed document, it works better than a cheap copier and costs less than the commercial service.

Licenses, Dues, Miscellaneous Costs

Other monthly costs include rent, utilities, and telephone. There are usually up front costs like rental deposits and telephone installation costs, from both the local telephone company and the inside line installer. Some rental agreements provide an allowance for tenant improvements. If your proposed office needs them, ask about such a break.

You will probably need a business license from your local taxing authority, the city or county. Some municipalities may require a permit. We will cover this and other requirements in a later chapter. You may also want to incur the association dues and subscription costs of any professional organization you feel is necessary.

The counting-house of an accomplished merchant is a school of method where the great science may be learned of ranging particulars under generals, of bringing the different parts of a transaction together, and of showing at one view a long series of dealing and exchange.

—*Samuel Johnson (1709-1784)*

I recommend joining a professional association as soon as financially feasible. Besides the obvious benefits of maintaining professional competence through continuing professional education (CPE) courses and helping you network with others in the profession, many associations offer special group insurance rates and discounts on professional supplies and texts.

Among the kinds of group insurance rates offered are those for life, health, and errors and omissions insurance. We list and briefly describe a selection of professional associations in the Appendix at the back of this book. For a more complete list, scan the "Accounting" and "Taxation" sections of the *Encyclopedia of Associations* at your local public library.

Other Expenses for a "Knowledge Business"

To keep your clients from getting into serious tax difficulties you must give good advice. That means getting all the continuing education you can to improve your knowledge and to learn how clients can benefit from it. You may not enroll in much continuing education in the first year, but you will want a modest start-up library. Nowadays it is typically an "electronic library."

The Business Library

A modern and current library is as necessary in a bookkeeping and tax-preparation business as in a lawyer's office. Keeping abreast of changes in tax laws and regulations *is* the business. Until recently that meant subscribing to and reading one of the loose-leaf tax services. I subscribed to the Research Institute of America and Commerce Clearing House tax services. Over the years a practitioner could anticipate building an impressive library of perhaps 100 volumes. That is history.

About the only book I use is my handy desk reference, J.K. Lasser's *Your Income Tax*. Full-time or part-time start-up, you can acquire the latest edition at your nearest drugstore or discount office supply. I may own it only because I am old enough to find a certain tactile comfort and emotional security in flipping through printed pages. Everything else I need is on my computer screen from CD-ROM disks. They provide the information of several massive tax libraries in less space than half a dozen paperback books. I wouldn't be without them.

If you need up-to-the-minute information, you must turn to on-line tax services, which have been around for some time now. That market is in such flux today—with the changes occurring on the Internet and its commercial overlay, the World Wide Web, and with the interest in it of the telephone companies and other public carriers—that any service I name may also be history by the time you read this. The widest entree to tax services is probably via the Lexis-Nexis tax libraries accessible on the Internet or through a provider like America Online, Compuserve, and so on. In our area, Lexis-Nexis has set up low-cost public access through some county law libraries. If your county law library or other facility subscribes to Lexis-Nexis, you may want to drop by and scan its printed *Directory of On-Line Services*. The alphabetical and subject indexes together comprise over 400 8½-by-11-inch pages of small print. They list six pages of federal tax services and about five of state tax services. Mead Data Central, which owns Lexis-Nexis, can be telephoned at 1-800-426-7675.

Continuing Education and Credentials

Investing in knowledge also means studying and keeping up with developments in the profession. Your clients will expect—and you should give—the highest quality service you can manage. No matter what titles or designations you acquire, your work must be based on an internalized standard of good practice. Even the most impressive designation is never worth more than its owner's knowledge and integrity. The greater the knowledge and attention you apply to your clients' affairs, the more valuable your advice is and the more you should earn. That's how it should be, and, having said it, here is what some of the names and designations mean.

Certified Public Accountants

Certified public accountants are the most highly trained in the profession. They must undertake a lengthy course of study and pass the Uniform Certified Public Accountants Examination before their state will license them. The two-day examination is in five parts, covering accounting practice, theory, auditing, and business law. It is 60 percent multiple-choice and 40 percent written. Few examinees pass the first time, although passing at least two parts allows them to take the failed parts again. All CPAs are licensed by a state agency (see the Appendix) to handle complex tax, tax-appeal, accounting, and business-planning tasks. Most CPAs belong to the American Institute of Certified Public Accountants (AICPA) and adhere to its rules, ethical standards, procedures, and CPE requirements. A CPA might charge around $300 to complete a relatively uncomplicated tax return. Even the modestly wealthy taxpayer could anticipate a $2,000 to $4,000 CPA's bill.

Public Accountants

A "public accountant" is almost but not quite an anachronism. The term applies partly to a class of practitioners who were "grandfathered in" to practice under the laws and regulations enacted to govern CPAs. There are probably very few of them left these days. Most of the approximately 4,000 public accountants nationwide earned the designation by passing two parts of the CPA exam after one or two years' accounting experience.

When last I checked, 21 states, the District of Columbia, Puerto Rico, Guam, and the Virgin Islands let anyone set up as an "accountant." The other 29 states restrict the term's use to people they license as certified public accountants and public accountants.

In California, for example, only a CPA or public accountant can receive pay to perform an audit, examine, verify, investigate, present, or review financial transactions and accounting records—or do any tasks incidental to those activities—then certify such reports, etc., for publication in order to get credit or to file with a court or government agency, and so on. (California Business and Professions Code section 5051.)

When my young master has once got the skill of keeping accounts (which is a business of reason, more than arithmetic) perhaps it will not be amiss that his father from thenceforth require him to do it in all his concernments.

—John Locke (1632-1704)
"On Education"

Bookkeepers

Bookkeepers in this state can perform many services that would qualify as public accountancy but *only* if a CPA or public accountant did them. Thus, bookkeepers may keep books, make trial balances, prepare statements, make audits or prepare reports as part of bookkeeping operations for clients, prepare or sign tax returns as clients' tax preparer, prepare personal financial or investment plans or provide clients with products or others' services to implement personal financial or investment plans, and provide management consulting services. Despite all this latitude, however, I am very careful to correct people who refer to me as their accountant and to point out that I am a bookkeeper. Laws and regulations differ among the states, so you will have to see what bookkeepers may do where you live.

Many small-business owners and managers are too enmeshed in day-to-day operations to bother with even the most rudimentary company books. Most can't afford a CPA firm's services, and it would be uneconomical for them to hire one if they could. They are better served by bookkeepers, a cheaper choice and just as professional despite the lack of certification or licenses. A bookkeeper's standards are controlled ultimately by the marketplace, which can be as uncompromising a steward of quality as any there is. Bookkeeping is what I do, and I can build upon it as seems appropriate, taking or leaving whatever professional designations and titles suit the practice.

Thousands of bookkeepers working throughout the economy, independently and in every size company, keep the nation's business finances on track and provide needed services to hundreds of thousands of individuals. Many are better at personal tax law and practice than some CPAs, particularly those who specialize in corporate and advanced practice; and historically bookkeepers are the origin of the whole profession.

Enrolled Agents

A public accountant or bookkeeper can get an "enrolled agent" (EA) designation by passing a two-day IRS examination to qualify for representing clients before all administrative levels of the IRS in audit, appeal, and negotiation cases. Enrolled agents handle tax preparation and planning as well as bookkeeping for individuals and businesses. Even so, public accountants and EAs may be too expensive for the ordinary consumer or taxpayer.

Certified Financial Planners

An ostensibly new industry called personal financial planning arose in the mid-1980s. It included such diverse practitioners as investment advisers and counselors, securities dealers, lawyers, accountants, and insurance and real-estate salesmen. The specialty had been all but unnoticed for years. Its sudden visibility resulted in large part from several developments that created new opportunities and complexity in business and personal finance. First, there appeared an array of exceptional new financial instruments to augment the intricacy of estate planning, risk management, and personal investing. Further, new federal regulations permitted insurance companies and every kind of financial institution to enter each other's markets. The enormous opportunities these changes created transformed the occupational backwater of building and conserving wealth into a booming, hyper-charged business.

Eventually the Institute of Certified Financial Planners (ICFP) emerged as the predominant association to formalize and rationalize professional financial planning. Anyone who integrates it into a bookkeeping service —an option I will discuss later—may wish to consider a "Certified Financial Planner'' (CFP) designation. The institute, as a private association of financial planners, awards its designation to anyone who passes a series of examinations that deal with the instruments and techniques of financial planning. Membership is based on the institute's standards of education and ethical practice, and on satisfying annual CPE requirements.

The Meaning of All This

Whether or not you pursue the professional designations that suit your strengths and practice, I recommend taking all the CPE credits you can. Some states offer special certification based on such credits. California's former tax certification program was scrubbed for want of funding. Even without licensure or certification incentives, however, continuing education is a good idea. Courses are usually available from the professional associations and your state college system by correspondence, on videotape, in seminars, and at conferences. Once you are in the system you will receive copious notification of them.

These are necessary expenses and will cost you plenty, but if you want free information about changes in the federal tax code and forms, you can enroll in the federal Tax Practitioner Program by ordering Publication 1045 from your local IRS Area Distribution Center.* Participating gets you on the Tax Practitioner Mailing List for new forms and the IRS Newsletter. Your first order might include Publication 847, *Practice . . . before the IRS*, and Circular 320, *Regulations Governing . . . Practice before the IRS*. Publication 1045 also gives information about IRS documents available on CD-ROM and by modem access to its bulletin board service (BBS).

---

* Addresses for the three Area Distribution Centers are: IRS-EADC, P.O. Box 27322, Richmond, VA 23261-7322; IRS CADC, P.O. Box 8909, Bloomington, IL 61702-8909; and IRS-WADC, Rancho Cordova, CA 95743-0001.

From the Annals of Internal Revenue

One of the thorniest issues for the framers of the Constitution was how to generate income from a nation that had broken with Great Britain in part because of unjust taxes. Unsympathetic as some of them may have been to taxation, the framers had fresh memories of trying to raise an army and run a government on borrowed money. Their compromise was to give the central government "power to lay and collect taxes, duties, imposts and excises. . ." but with all duties, imposts and excises to be apportioned among the states and levied uniformly throughout them.

Congress's preference ran to customs and tariffs, which it hoped would also discourage imports and protect new industries. Alexander Hamilton, a strong federalist and first Secretary of the Treasury, prevailed upon it, nonetheless, to set up a system of excise taxes and an organization to collect them. These met with great disfavor and led to an armed confrontation, the Whisky Rebellion of 1794, in which federal troops put down a group of farmers who had taken up arms in defiance of the tax.

Thomas Jefferson—elected third President on an agrarian and less-government platform—got Congress to repeal all internal taxes and run the government on tariffs alone. That worked only until the War of 1812.

Repeatedly throughout our history, the sudden need for large sums to fight a major war has radically changed our tax system. In 1812 Congress levied a direct income tax on each of the 18 states and set up our first sales tax, on luxury goods like jewelry and silverware. Congress abolished the income tax in 1817 and along with it, for the second time since Hamilton, the office of Commissioner of Internal Revenue.

It is better to have too much computer capacity than not enough. You will make your money on performance, and this is not the place to over-economize.

4

Computers and Software

A S I mentioned earlier, if you had set up as a bookkeeper and tax preparer a few years ago, the processing services would have contacted you with their form-processing deals. You could check at your bank and with colleagues to find them, but typically the services would come looking for you. You would give them your calculations and get back finished returns to file for your clients.

All that has changed. Using a calculator and pencil to keep books or figure returns for a batch processor is tolerable only briefly and with very few clients. If you start out in bookkeeping by doing things by hand as I did, it rapidly gets very burdensome. Today "rapidly" means almost instantly. The wizardry available in computer accounting software makes manual bookkeeping an unacceptable choice except in the very beginning. Getting into the business seriously means getting computerized. Start-up capital for hardware and software would be in the neighborhood of $2,500 to $5,000, depending mainly on the power of the hardware.

Computers are essential in this business, and this whole chapter will be devoted to them. First off, they build customer credibility. The public, with the exception of fewer and fewer elderly clients, has become accustomed to them and expects to see laser-printed output from us. My older clients often were intimidated by computers. They seemed to distrust them and were uncomfortable with them. For that reason, I didn't have one on my desk for years. But all clients these days expect a high-quality electronic product for their fees, and even the older ones have come to accept the sight and sound of a computer on the desk.

Shopping for Hardware

To do any bookkeeping at all today, you *need* adequate hardware and the requisite software. Don't hold back; get it. Technology is evolving so fast that you have to pick a time to enter this market and get the best hardware you can. Whatever you buy today, something more gee-whiz will come along within the next six months. It's a fact you have to live with. Just be sure that the equipment will run the software you need and will provide some opportunity for expansion. I will get a little technical in this chapter about how much microprocessor speed and RAM and hard disk memory you need, but it will probably be out of date before these pages reach you. The rules don't change, however, so the current technology I mention here briefly is only to illustrate the rules. A few years down the line they may serve as a sort of reference point.

Begin to think about computer equipment early and give it a lot of thought. A computer is a way to amplify your own brainpower and energy; it is a tool. If the computer, its software, or peripheral equipment will not save or make you money, don't buy it.

An old rule of computer buying was to select the software first, then get the computer to run it. The rule still applies, but hardware specifications have converged so much that if you buy as much computer as you can afford, with plenty of capacity left over to expand, you can handle any software. There are qualifications, however, which I will discuss below.

On to the basic equipment. I feel that full-size desktop computers are mandatory. Laptops and notebooks still seem to be in the "expensive fun" category. The basic rule is to get the biggest, fastest equipment available in your price range. It will be too small and slow soon enough.

None of us know enough about the equipment to buy it without an expert's help. If you don't have someone you normally deal with, do some research. You could look over recent computer magazines and books to pick up the language and get a rough idea of what is available to serve your needs. It is a good preparation for talking to an expert. The books are almost certainly out of date, and the magazines soon will be. There probably is not an unbiased analysis of equipment in any of the magazines. The ads are eye-openers. Prices are all over the map, mostly highly discounted. Mail-order computer prices, however, seldom include technical support beyond what comes over the telephone line.

Hands-on technical support is essential. Past a certain point most of us are computer illiterates. If, like me, you feel uncomfortable with your own computer knowledge, you need a local provider. Without a considerable background in personal computers, we can all benefit from professional help to purchase and set up the system. True, you will pay more for the equipment and service, at least for initial set-up and installation, but in the long run you will be ahead in terms of maintenance and support for that bleak day when your equipment goes AWOL.

To find an expert, talk to all the professionals you know, not just other bookkeeper/tax preparers. If you have to look in the Yellow Pages for computer consultants or suppliers, ask them for references.

Talk to all of the references you can. Ask embarrassing questions. Are they satisfied with prices and service? Did they change from a service they were dissatisfied with? Which one? How reliable and prompt is the service? How good is it? Is there a wide choice of equipment? Can you mix and match with non-house brands? How user-friendly is the operating system installed? Is the customer at the mercy of the machine after the provider sets it up or is the operating system accessible without getting in trouble? Is the provider more interested in selling high-priced equipment and software than getting the customer the best deal? Does the provider speak English or cyber-jargon? Is the provider intimidating? If this provider quit business tomorrow, could another firm take over the contract without any changes in your equipment?

As almost everyone knows, there are two major kinds of computers today: the Apple Macintosh, or Mac, and the PC, or what used to be called the IBM PC. Without doing a promotion for either the Macintosh or PC, my personal impression is that the PC dominates business. Although interfaces and exchanges between the Mac and PC are easier than ever, and although by almost every measure the Mac is a better machine, business preferences and business software run to the PC. And, for that inevitable day when you have to exchange electronic data with a colleague or a government agency, you will have fewer problems if you stick with a PC. While Apple's new PowerMac (which can outperform PCs on PC turf) does fit the category, it currently tends to be more expensive because it also has Mac software capabilities. At this writing, too, Apple is struggling to maintain its already slim market share and has a negligible business presence.

Bench-built PCs, assembled locally by the neighborhood techies, often match or surpass many name brands. There are also small high-quality manufacturers that build to outstanding specifications. But, no matter how good the provider or the machine's specs are, stick with established brands such as Compaq, Hewlett-Packard, IBM, Gateway 2000, and Dell. All of these have dependable warranties and good service contracts. They're likelier to be around when you need them.

When you buy, buy for tomorrow. Keep an eye on upgrading the system's capabilities in the future. Ask if it can be upgraded; increasingly the machines are being built with that in mind. The best machines are adaptable to new technology so you don't have to throw them out and start all over again. A skilled provider can, if you wish, install new electronics in the existing computer case for much less than a new machine. The high-end models with ample power supplies and cooling adapt better than entry-level machines. Even so, long before the machine wears out it will be obsolete, and you'll probably want to buy the next generation to benefit from the greater power. Use the same rule for trading up as buying: do so when it saves or makes you money.

With that rule in mind, remember that in terms of computing capacity and software capability, it is better to have too much memory than not enough, better to have the fastest CPU (central processing unit) chip on the market, and better to have full-featured, complicated software that handles whatever comes along. At the time of this writing (actually, a rewriting in late 1998), there is a choice of CPUs. Intel Corporation's Pentium II chip predominates, but Intel also sells a cheaper, slightly lower-grade "Celeron" chip to compete with chips from Advanced Micro Design (AMD) and Cyrix Corporation. As a result, computer prices have fallen dramatically. Our experts recommend several of the competing CPUs: a midrange Pentium II CPU that runs at at least 333 megahertz (Mhz) or, alternatively, Intel's Celeron 333 MHz or AMD's K6-2. Sixty-four megabytes of random access memory (RAM) is a minimum for all realistic purposes. RAM chips store temporary memory until the machine is turned off. You'll want "cache" memory of 512 kilobytes to speed operations, but 128 are enough for the more efficient Celeron chip. Get at least a four-gigabyte hard disk and a 56K modem designated V.90. These are basic specifications for 1998 but they should remain a brief guide for a few months and be a starting point for later.

One of the oldest illustrations of business activity shows clerks in 1518 doing their calculations on the abacus. The profession always had good reason to pioneer in technology.

Remember, you will make money on performance, and this is not the place to over-economize. I will explain soon why current software dictates loading up on permanent and temporary memory.

Choosing Software

Earlier I mentioned buying the machine to match the software. Computer software programs or applications "launch" from a "platform" called an operating system (OS) or disk operating system (DOS). In fact until very recently the operating program for the PC, or IBM-compatible, machine was mainly Microsoft's DOS: MS-DOS or just DOS.

Software Launch Pads

Until a few years ago, PC programs ran on DOS. Today current programs run only as Windows applications. In a way that's a pity because Windows and most of its applications are memory hogs. Both hard-disk and RAM memory are cheap today, but it still means you have to buy much more machine to do what once you could do on less. For example, one professional tax preparation program in DOS used two megabytes of hard disk space and two megabytes of RAM but in Windows it took five megabytes of hard disk memory and minimally four megabytes of RAM (eight recommended).

Microsoft's latest version, Windows 98, like the Mac's operating system, is only the most visible element of computer industry's efforts to make computers a simple home appliance. Soundblaster cards and hi-fi speakers are another. Essentially, computers have changed from tools to toys, or at least a tool buried inside a toy. There is simply a larger market for toys than tools, just as IBM discovered in the 1950s that there was a greater business than scientific market for computers. The price of developing the new Windows-based environment for fun and games, however, has been to require of every new computer a voracious and otherwise unneeded appetite for hard-disk and RAM memory. I'd advise making sure you can at least quadruple your machine's 64 MB of RAM.

Unfortunately, for those of us content to purchase a tool and get on with our business there is little choice. Even if the DOS version attracts or attracted you by being lean and efficient (my own preference), prepare to acquire, and get used to, the Windows version.

I have a few final observations on today's computers and the new Windows system. Windows' advantage is that it uses a more efficient 32-bit command architecture that runs several programs at once better than its prior versions did. Windows' disadvantage is that controlling it increasingly requires rolling a plastic shell called a mouse around on whatever free desk space you have and "clicking" when an arrow points to "icons" (pictures) on the screen. This is not only slower and a nuisance for typists, but is more than a little retrograde. The reason why the Phoenicians invented the alphabet was in order to communicate better than with pictures. It is still possible to use keystrokes to execute most commands in most programs, although that's becoming a steeper uphill battle. I recommend learning and using key commands exclusively, if you can, simply for the added speed when tax season arrives. In short, I would be very content, despite "progress" to the contrary, to have the 32-bit architecture without reverting to cartoons, hieroglyphics, and pointers. Also, you won't need soundblaster cards and speakers but finding a computer for business these days without them is more trouble than it's worth. Two megabytes of video memory is a minimum requirement; but don't worry, four are pretty standard now.

Accounting Software

Software becomes obsolete faster than hardware. Good programs are displaced by better ones. Mediocre software may take on new life. Much of the software I mention now may soon be out of date or significantly changed; it doesn't even merit appendix space. Ads in the professional journals will remain the best source for finding available programs.

Nowadays Intuit's *Quicken* or *Quick Books* will handle the average small business's books. If you find yourself with a corporate client with elaborate levels of subsidiaries and diverse profit centers, you will have to look for big-time software to handle the complexity. But for ordinary purposes I find that *Quicken/QuickBooks/QuickBooks Pro* are fine.

That's today, of course. One general aid for selecting software in this evolving universe is to look for the availability of add-ons, add-ins, templates, and retrofits for a program. Usually you find these in classified ads in the back of trade journals. They gauge a program's success and popularity. In choosing a software package, popularity may win out over grades from a laboratory test. This is especially true where the programs are fairly similar and competitive. First, your business is not a laboratory, and you will enjoy the advantage of accessories that other people have developed for the most popular brands of software. I have also heard criticisms of how "objective" magazine tests are of their advertisers' products. You shouldn't ignore the tests and critical comments, but there is usually a good reason for a program's popularity. Second, buying the winner in the marketplace is a way to avoid what may become orphan software, whose files or templates you can never exchange with, or get from, other practitioners and which may become obsolete while more competitive brands are revised and upgraded. The rule, in short, is to buy what everyone else like you is buying.

Tax-Preparation Software

The rule also applies to business-oriented applications like tax-preparation software. Increasingly, this software appears on CD-ROM bundled with tax laws, regulations, and instructions keyed to the tax form displayed on the screen. It will help to consult with colleagues about which software they use, then to do careful research. Again, these are programs available at time of writing. Things may have changed radically by the time you read this. Meanwhile, here is a look at some current tax-preparation software.

Lacerte Software, which I use, suits my needs very well. The company's entire output is available on floppy disks or on a CD-ROM, with all of its programs downloadable from the CD on a pay-as-you-go basis. If you wish, you can process returns directly from the CD-ROM, and save hard-disk space for your most used programs. All the programs are updated with periodic CD releases. Prior-year programs are archived on a single CD-ROM. All federal tax calculations are integrated with whatever state form programs you purchase.

The *Lacerte* program runs from pull-down menus, and its commands are mostly single-letter strokes. The program is set up for federal and

---

Facing Page:

Form 1040 was substantially redesigned in tax year 1944 and many of its design features—areas for exemptions, income, tax computation, and tax due or refund—remain in use. A one-third page W-2 withholding receipt was tried for tax years 1944 through 1947, but the 1040A replaced it in tax year 1948. The 1040A (shown here) was converted to a two-sided punch card for 1954, and spaces were added to enter both spouses' Social Security Numbers.

U. S. INDIVIDUAL INCOME TAX RETURN — 1954

Read instructions carefully.
Complete both sides of form.
Please print.

U. S. INDIVIDUAL INCOME TAX RETURN — **1954**

If you use this form, the Internal Revenue Service will compute your tax.

U. S. TREASURY DEPARTMENT / INTERNAL REVENUE SERVICE

1. NAME

2. WIFE'S (HUSBAND'S) NAME

3. HOME ADDRESS (NUMBER AND STREET OR RURAL ROUTE)

(CITY, TOWN, OR POST OFFICE) (ZONE) (STATE)

4. (Check) ☐ Single ☐ Married

5. Is this a joint return? ☐ Yes ☐ No

6. Is wife (husband) filing separately? ☐ Yes ☐ No

	Taxpayer's	Your Wife's (Husband's)
7. Social Security No.		
8. Wages	(a)	(b)
9. Tax Withheld	(a)	(b)
10. Other Income	(a)	(b)
11. Special Credit	(a)	(b)
12. Exclusion	(a)	(b)

Only if joint return

• List your exemptions on other side.

Do not bend, pin, or mutilate. ENCLOSE FORMS W-2

I DECLARE UNDER THE PENALTIES OF PERJURY THAT THIS IS A TRUE, CORRECT, AND COMPLETE RETURN TO THE BEST OF MY KNOWLEDGE AND BELIEF.

(FOR USE OF INTERNAL REVENUE SERVICE)
C   B
T   R

TAXPAYER'S SIGNATURE AND DATE | IF JOINT RETURN, WIFE'S (HUSBAND'S) SIGNATURE

FORM 1040A

---

13. EXEMPTIONS FOR YOURSELF AND WIFE (OR HUSBAND)   EXEMPTIONS

(a) For your own exemption, write the FIGURE 1 ⟶

(b) If you were 65 or over at the end of 1954, write the FIGURE 1 ⟶

(c) If taxpayer was blind at the end of 1954, write the FIGURE 1 ⟶

(d) If your wife (or husband) had no income in 1954, or if this is a joint return, write the FIGURE 1 for her (or his) exemption ⟶

(e) If she (or he) is claimed as an exemption in (d) above and was 65 or over at the end of 1954, write the FIGURE 1 ⟶

(f) If she (or he) is claimed as an exemption in (d) above and was blind at the end of 1954, write the FIGURE 1 ⟶

14. EXEMPTIONS FOR YOUR CHILDREN AND OTHER DEPENDENTS (List below)

Name (also give address if different from yours) ● Enter Figure 1 in the last column to right for each name listed.	Relationship	Answer ONLY for dependents other than children		
		Did dependent have gross income of $600 or more?	Amount YOU spent for dependent's support. If 100%, write "All"	Amount spent by OTHERS including dependent
				⟶
				⟶
				⟶
				⟶
				⟶

15. Enter total number of exemptions listed in items 13 and 14 above. ⟶

state electronic filing. Like many professional tax programs today, *Lacerte* integrates a number of federal income tax calculations with those for state forms. Among them are calculations for child care credits, self-employment tax, standard mileage versus actual expenses, and IRA and Keogh deductions, as well as calculations in some of the less commonly used tax forms.

When you can't or don't want to purchase software for each type of return, *Lacerte* offers remote-entry processing of any state or federal form via modem at a per-return charge. In fact, you can also pay a deposit and use the entire *Lacerte* program remotely on a pay-per-return basis. It can be a real advantage for smaller or start-up practices. The program will import data from popular accounting programs and export tax return data to the Bureau of National Affairs (BNA) *Tax Planner* program, which helps make federal and state income tax projections and calculations for up to 10 years.

Lacerte offers training and update seminars, good technical support, and CPE courses. The program is DOS-based and will run on MS-DOS 5.0 or above using two-thirds (2/3!) of a megabyte of RAM, with as little as 12MB of hard-disk space.

Because I use this software I know it and am biased in its favor. It costs $1,250 for the federal individual 1040 income tax program, with those for one, two or three states available at $150, $200, or $250 respectively. Additional federal forms for partnerships, corporations, S-corporations and fiduciary income taxes cost $650 per module, with state forms available for $100 each. Lacerte Software Corporation is at 4835 LBJ Parkway, Suite 1000, Dallas, TX 75244; 800-765-7777.

There are half a dozen or more other professional level tax and accounting programs that other practitioners find acceptable and use. I don't know about them other than by word of mouth and promotional materials. I have listed a few in the Appendix along with what I understand are good-quality consumer programs. They are worth your consideration. In any event, don't take my word alone. There are plenty of programs on the market. More appear every year, and others disappear. Take your time to test and try as many as you can. Get demonstration disks, ask questions, talk to others in the business, keep your own inclinations in mind, wait, and then decide. Your software will be a major investment. Once you start to use a program it is very difficult to switch. Don't make your software investment decision hastily.

For example, one prominent program in the Appendix, *TAASCforce*, is a high-quality product designed by CPAs to be used as stand-alone or integrated modules. Using the entire program ensures complete compatibility among all accounting, client write-up, and tax functions. While an excellent choice for some, it may be either too powerful or too inflexible for others. It is more than I need but may suit you. The decision is not easy, but if you take your time you will make the right choice.

In addition, there is now an updated batch processing service with a startling option that deserves mention here in the text. Starting in 1996, with the 1995 tax year, clients of Compucraft Data Services (17002 South Prairie Avenue, Torrance, CA 90504; 800-435-7829) were able to transmit data to the company's main frame computer over a toll-free line and get back a finished return, usually in less than two minutes, for printing out in the office. Turn-around is limited only by the speed of your modem. In one test conducted in October 1995, 10 complex returns transmitted from a 486-based PC with a 14,400-bps modem (not the fastest—see below) were calculated and sent back in under three minutes.

The advantages of near-instant electronic batch processing over a stand-alone program are: there is no up-front software expense other than a \$9.95 shipping and handling fee for communications software; you pay only for returns actually processed; the company updates its program continuously and you need never override calculation results until the next update arrives; the company automatically backs up data off-site at its facilities; you can complete interview forms and calculate tax estimates, including what-if scenarios, before going on-line; toll-free technical support can view a return while it is on-line; as an alternative, the company can print the return and ship you the hard copy along with a presentation folder and filing envelopes or it can file the return electronically, after first analyzing it for correctness; and finally, if your office system crashes, you can do it the old-fashioned way and send a hard copy of the interview forms for the company to key, calculate, print, collate, and send back.

Compucraft's software, *In-House Plus* (DOS), free except for shipping and handling, includes federal individual returns and those for Arizona, California, Colorado, Hawaii, Illinois, and Oregon, as well as Partnership, Corporation, S-Corporation, and Amended return processing and Electronic filing forms. The company also offers a \$35 program, *PC Shorts*, to process simple returns in-house. The batch processing fee of \$15 each for up to 50 returns drops to \$10 for over 200 and down to \$8.50 above 500. Two-thirds of the company's clients feel they save time and labor by paying the company to print and ship back the returns.

While this approach lacks many of the bells and whistles of high-end software, its support, simplicity, and cost-effectiveness may make it worth considering, especially for start-up firms and even for established practitioners. Just call or write, and all these companies will cheerfully send you their sales information.

Peripherals, Possibilities, and a Warning

Besides handling bookkeeping and tax preparation tasks, a computer can streamline your work, give you a competitive edge, and make your business more productive and profitable. It can help with client write-up work, electronic spreadsheets, and amortization and depreciation schedules; it can handle your word processing for letters, newsletters, and announcements; it can keep time and billing records; it can provide a client database to manipulate in different ways for mailing lists; and it will run elaborate reminder calendars. It expands both the kind and quantity of work you do.

Sold on computers? I couldn't work without one.

File Back-Up Hardware

First, here is the warning. Back up your files! My meager understanding of computers is that they work in tiny, spooky flickers of electricity. It can take very little—just a blip of static—for all your work to vanish without even a puff of smoke. Also, your hard disk's eventual failure is as certain as death and—well—taxes. Floppy disks are so cheap that every client's file can live on one or perhaps several of them. Zip and Syquest disks hold hundreds of times more. Tape back-up systems are designed to back up the data from the entire hard drive. If you rotate three copies from the computer to office-storage to home, your records are never more than two days old, and at least one tape (or Zip, etc., disk) is safe from all but Armageddon. A second hard drive is a possibility but doesn't evade disaster like this three-step rotation.

Take the same kind of care if you monkey with the machine's innards. It takes only a little stray static electricity to reduce a valuable chip or circuit board to a sheet of coppery resin and pebbles.

CD-ROM Drives

Like most computer peripherals and equipment, CD-ROM drives have gotten much cheaper and better since their introduction. They now run routinely at "32x" speeds, 32 times faster than originally—a real advantage for searching data on disk. The drives play either the naked disk or spin it inside a protective carrier called a "carousel." Carousels suit an office where many people use the disk and often insert and remove it from the drive. See your computer provider about which drive will best fit your needs.

A CD-ROM drive is a must. You can pack several libraries of tax information in the space of half a dozen small books. You will need all the current information you can get to provide your customers with the best tax information available, and you can't do it more efficiently than on CD-ROM disks.

Also, CD-ROM drives let you benefit from new software packaging in which providers put *all* their applications on one disk. It is the pay-as-you-go feature I mentioned before. Buy one program and you get a disk with everything on it. To buy more just telephone in your registration and credit card numbers to pay for a code to unlock and download any program on the disk. Manuals are shipped separately.

Blessed are they who back up their files, for they shall be saved.

—Anonymous Back-up Tape Drive Salesman

Laser Printers

Print your reports on the best laser printer you can find. Like mechanical dot-matrix printers—which are not acceptable for tax returns—laser printers build letters on the page with closely packed dots. They project tiny points of light onto a photocopy drum, the "print engine," which rolls the image onto paper exactly like a copier. Canon Corporation makes the engines for Hewlett-Packard and most other laser printers. The dots on older laser printers were packed together at 300-by-300 dots per square inch. Close up or with a reading glass, you can see the jagged edges these dots make on the letters. Many newer laser printers print at 1200 (dpi), and the dots all but invisible. No one except high-quality graphics publishers, however, needs resolution higher than 600 dpi—and 300 dpi is perfectly acceptable if that's what you have.

Hewlett-Packard pioneered and retains a lead in laser printing. My understanding is that other printers emulate the H-P standard to one degree or another. Consequently, an application's printing commands are usually written to that standard. The closer your printer emulates the H-P "command architecture" the fewer problems you will have printing from any program. Good quality laser printers sell in a range of prices that depend on quality and how fast they print.

How *fast* you need to print will depend on how *much* you need to print. In tax season that may mean the fastest on the market. Most of the year four to six pages a minute may be fine. My printer runs at eight pages a minute. Newer printers are much faster. Keep the seasonal rush in mind; speed matters, and this is another place not to over-economize. If you do, you may regret it in the middle of the night when you are waiting for old faithful to puff out another page.

Fax-Modems

A fax-modem may work for you better than a fax machine (which is a computer chip hooked up to a telephone and usually a cheap printer). But then you'll probably also need a scanner. All fax-modems run in the background while you are using the computer for something else. For faxes after hours you will have to leave your computer on to receive and store them. Don't worry, the CPU draws very little power. Just turn off the monitor and printer when you leave. Your hard disk will live longer, too, if you are not turning it on and off every day. As mentioned earlier, good modern fax-modems distinguish between voice and digital information, and may thus eliminate the need for an extra phone line. Some even offer caller identification and security, cue callers to leave a message, and will page you. Most can be remotely configured. A modem also lets you transfer data files between computers. Standard transmission speed these days is 56,000 bauds per second (bps), and it is essential to get one that conforms to what is called a V.90 standard. At the time of this writing the features available in modems were increasing enormously to handle a variety of communications needs with extreme simplicity. And even with increasing communication by e-mail over the Internet, faxes still serve best to transfer formatted documents.

Finally, modems are indispensable for filing returns electronically. At first, the IRS was very exacting about who filed by wire and how they did it. Since then it has made the procedure increasingly easy. For the IRS, electronic filing means less paper to deal with; for the client, it can mean a faster refund. Almost all tax preparation software contains an electronic filing utility. Not all of them may work as promised, but the IRS has a list of acceptable stand-alone utilities. If you process returns remotely via a service like *Lacerte* or *Computax*, the service will file electronically for you. Remember, however, that you will still need hard copies for the client and your files.

Final Words

Get a good monitor; it's easier on the eyes, especially when you have a tax form with fine print squeezed onto the screen. It should have a dot pitch of 0.28 millimeter or smaller. Be sure it's a non-interlaced screen, which flickers less. Screen size should be large—these days that's 17 inches—for easy readability. They cost almost three times as much as standard 15-inch monitors—as high as $700 compared to $250—but you will be looking at the screen for hours on end. Flat-screen LCD monitors are the future and are very superior. For the moment they're too costly, so wait until they're competitive with today's now obsolecent cathode ray tubes. The four-megabyte video card in most computers today will speed screen display far beyond anything you'll probably need.

There are other exciting and attractive computer possibilities, but limit your purchases to the essentials. At the moment, for example, there is a flurry of interest in all-in-one fax-printer-copier-scanner machines. My own feeling is that these are probably not the electronic Swiss Army Knives their manufacturers promise. Like every other compromise, they probably will do a score of things but none of them very well. They could be a suitable back-up in the reception room but would probably fail as the office workhorse in most of their multiple functions.

The message is: Buy fancy add-ons and gadgets only when they will pay for themselves with increased efficiency, and when you are sure they will work as you hope—not become expensive white elephants.

From the Annals of Internal Revenue

Despite periodic pleas from the Treasury Department and elsewhere, the federal government supported itself on tariffs for the 45 years following 1817. It took the Civil War to revive internal taxes, including another income tax.

Today's Internal Revenue Service had its beginnings on July 1, 1862, when President Lincoln signed into law the nation's most sweeping tax measure to that date. It established a new office of Commissioner of Internal Revenue and created the model for our modern system of taxation. The income tax was progressive in nature, imposing three percent on incomes over $600 but less than $10,000 annually, and five percent on any income over $10,000.

Lincoln selected George S. Boutwell, a 44-year-old Massachusetts lawyer, to be his Commissioner of Internal Revenue. Boutwell had served in the Massachusetts legislature and as governor, and later would serve in both the House of Representatives and the Senate and as Secretary of the Treasury. In less than eight months Boutwell organized a field and office force, contracted to print revenue stamps, drafted regulations, and constructed the framework for today's Internal Revenue Service.

The new revenue act permitted the President to divide the country into collection districts and, with the Senate's advice and consent, to appoint an assessor and collector for each district. The assessor listed objects of taxation and presented his list to the collector. The lists were the collector's warrant for payment of taxes. Within 20 days of receiving the assessor's lists, the collector was to notify taxpayers by newspaper ads and posted notices to pay in person or by mail. The collector could seize and sell the assets of delinquent taxpayers. It was a system that proved hazardous to collectors, particularly in the far west.

As a beginner without any special advantages it does help to identify yourself and your market right away as middle-of-the-road for people who work for wages and small-business people.

Finding Your Market

A FEW books and experts warn that it is as hard for a bookkeeper to start in a new location as it is for any new professional. Lacking personal and business contacts makes it very difficult to get those first few clients. For a variety of reasons you also may lack sufficient personal and business contacts to set up where you are. If so, you might as well search your state or the whole nation for a place to start business. You can look anywhere and might even consider a smaller town. Before you move, however, you had better be sure the market is there to support you.

Where Is Your Market?

It takes around 75 to 100 clients to support a one-person bookkeeping firm. Many of those clients will be wage earners and small businesses. Even if you plan to set up in your present community, do a little homework. The place to start is at your public library. Your decision will not be purely economic. The choice will reflect your business plan and your personal preferences. Location will also influence the kind of client you get. In a retirement community you will get local businesses and senior citizens; in an industrial center you will get merchants, truckers, small manufacturers or suppliers, and wage earners.

Pick some likely places, either those you know and would like to live in, or those that other people have rated as good places to live and work in. Base your choice on sound market research and the kind of lifestyle you want. The standard indexes are *Cities of the United States* and the *Statistical Abstract of the United States*. These will give population trends, average incomes, and major industries. You might also look at *Forbes* magazine's annual ratings of cities and Savageau & Boyer's *Places Rated Almanac*. If you can't find these, check for similar guides in the catalog at your local public library under the subject heading "Cities and Towns—United States—Ratings." Also investigate general economic conditions, trends of local industries, and major employers. Contact the local U.S. Department of Commerce field office or SBA field office.

"Wha's there?"
"It's me, you dom scoundrel!" said the frenzied merchant; "ye've added up the year of our Laird with the pounds."

> —*"The Rich Merchant by Bookkeeping,"*
> KNICKERBOCKER MAGAZINE
> *December 1845, p. 583*

A community's total number of businesses—including manufacturers, wholesalers, retailers, and services—is a better index than is population of likely economic activity. When you get that number from the Department of Commerce, SBA, business licenses at the County Recorder's Office, or local Chamber of Commerce, cut it roughly in half to account for the businesses with good enough books to lack an incentive to retain your services, for those that have their own bookkeeping person or department, or those that are too small to afford an outside service. You can find the ratio of bookkeepers to businesses by looking up "Bookkeeping Service" and "Tax Return Preparation" in the Yellow Pages. One bookkeeper to 50 potential business clients is a good ratio. Some localities have a ratio of one to 25, but this tends toward crowding. A ratio of one to 75 or 100 businesses could mean that the community may support additional services. Many eligible businesses don't use a bookkeeping service because they don't know the advantages of doing so. In the 40-year-old survey of how businesses kept books, cited in Chapter 1, participants felt that educating businesses to the value of bookkeeping services could reduce the ratio to one to 25. Also, ratios alone don't indicate the quality of competition. Skilled people can succeed in places that look crowded, and poor practitioners can fail in apparently good localities.

You need to do qualitative research, part of which requires investigating general economic conditions and the trends of local industries and major employers. This information should be available at the U.S. Department of Commerce field office, SBA field office, and other public and private sources in the area. Here is a checklist of questions that the information should cover.

What are government attitudes toward growth?

Is there a Chamber of Commerce to encourage business development?

Are industrial or agricultural conditions good?

Is the local economic trend up, down, or static?

Is the source of community wealth diversified and varied or a single industry?

Are income sources cyclical or steady?

Are major industries old and well established, young and growing, or new and risky?

Are the major industries stable or subject to wide fluctuations?

Is the community's economic outlook promising, uncertain, poor?

Is population growing, static, declining, aging?

What is per capita income?

Are transportation facilities, banking facilities, schools, and public services good, adequate, poor?

Are civic associations aggressive, adequate, stagnant, poor?

Have you canvassed the community to determine the number of bookkeeping services already operating the type you plan?

Have any bookkeeping services like yours closed recently? Why?

Are existing bookkeeping services busy? Do they serve local business adequately?

Are competitors well established?

Do competitors leave an opening because they are not serving part of the community, or because you are alert and aggressive?

Will competition be strong, active, weak, sluggish?

What do business and service clubs, the chamber of commerce, and others think of the prospects for another bookkeeping service in the community?

Have you talked to a banker, lawyer, or independent accountant? What are their opinions about your plan?

When you narrow your search, you will have to go look at the community if you are not already there. Then you will need to evaluate the answers you get to these questions. It is easier to judge your own community with these questions than to use the checklist for an unfamiliar one. This is a lot of work, but it is an excellent way to get all the cheap knowledge you can in order to avoid those expensive and unpleasant experiences later on.

Much of this information is available by writing and telephoning. If you are willing to dig, you can find the data. Once you start your research it will lead you to new sources. Here is where to begin looking:

Retail and wholesale businesses can provide advice and information about the immediate trading area.

If you belong to a community service club like Rotary, Lions, etc., attend the local chapter's meeting to learn about business in the community.

Newspaper circulation managers can provide advice and information about population, economic conditions, and businesses; newspaper advertising managers may be willing to provide a list of commercial and industrial prospects from their own advertising lists (but don't count on it).

Radio and television stations can provide information on the trading area.

Credit bureaus can provide current information on financial characteristics of an area and its residents.

Chambers of commerce can provide an analysis of local consumers and types of businesses.

Banks can provide wide range of data including credit ratings and general business conditions.

Public recorders and licensing agencies can provide information on construction permits that will show where and how many new homes and businesses will be built.

Directory services, local buyers' guides, and the Yellow Pages will provide lists of different commercial and industrial prospects.

Farm agents and farm organizations can provide information on farmers in the area as well as general information on their members.

Producers' cooperatives know their members very well and can also provide information on them and local business conditions.

Trade associations can provide market data and membership information.

Federal, state, and local government agencies can provide a range of statistics about specific areas.

Don't think of the community as a single town or an entire large city. The geographical size of your market is defined by how convenient it is to visit your clients, or for them to visit you. That may be a 10- to 15-mile radius from your office. It may be more. Some bookkeepers work where several small towns are clustered close together. A cluster like this should include, at a minimum, one town with at least 100 businesses. That is my situation. My office is in a town of about 5,000 people and some 600 businesses. There are several outlying towns and crossroads with firms and individuals I also serve. A situation like this may be worth looking into where one community is a great place to live while another is a bustling commercial center (but maybe you wouldn't want to live there).

Who Will Your Clients Be?

The ideal client, and one to seek from the outset, is the kind who knows enough about business affairs to recognize the importance of the service you are offering and who will let you do your job without a lot of meddling or anxiety. This kind of client—the most profitable, incidentally—is the most sought after and subject to the most competition.

As an upstart, you will be obliged to take less profitable, less desirable work.

Starting out, the clientele is just about anyone who comes through the door, usually individuals and small businesses. This is a fact of economic life until you establish yourself and can screen clients better, focusing on one kind of client as opposed to another. I don't recommend specializing, at least not at first. A beginner has to be a bit of a generalist, until acquiring a sufficient client base and experience to permit identifying the best kinds of clients to cultivate and which to let go.

As a beginner without any special advantages it does help to identify yourself and your market right away as middle-of-the-road for working people and young families: people who work for wages and small-business people. If you shoot for the low end of the market you will be in direct competition with H&R Block, one of the biggest franchises in the country, and they have that end of the market covered. Also the low end of the market produces more troublesome, less desirable clients. Clients who shop for low-cost bookkeeping services are more fixed on price than on service or on operating their businesses well. As I will point out later, you are not offering a price-sensitive product and should not try to compete on that basis. Also, be very leery of those who, when coming to you for the first time, reveal that they have had four different tax preparers in the last four years. There is probably a good—no, a bad —reason for that. At least contact those preparers before agreeing to take the client.

To some extent, office location will influence who your clients are. If a portion of your clientele includes senior citizens, they may ask you to do simple things like balance checkbooks, even write checks. It means acting as more of a service bureau than strictly as a bookkeeper. Serving seniors with checkbook monitoring and balancing may be a niche worth exploring, especially in a major retirement center.

Some individual clients will have small businesses and you may find yourself preparing taxes and doing bookkeeping for both. If the practice advances you may branch out, doing tax and bookkeeping work for other business entities like partnerships and perhaps small corporations. Potential commercial clients include new businesses, existing firms that appreciate the need for bookkeeping services, and those that are dissatisfied with their present records.

Lots of small-business people dislike working with printed forms and reporting requirements of any kind. They are eager to turn this work over to someone else. Many just don't know that yet. They often lack a disinterested person to discuss their management and financial problems with. These are areas where you can provide a valuable service.

You may have to go out and persuade some businesses that they need a good set of records. It's a selling job. It means inquiring whether a firm already uses an outside bookkeeper and, if not, why not. For instance, the services you offer could include taking over the client's tax reporting burden and filing the quarterly reports for estimated income tax, social security and withholding taxes. Your major services would include filing tax forms, routine bookkeeping, and making up operating statements.

Never ask of money spent
Where the spender thinks it went.
Nobody was ever meant
To remember or invent
What he did with every cent.

—Robert Frost (1874-1963)
"The Hardship of Accounting," 1936

Above a certain size, every business too small to have a full time bookkeeper is a potential client. The obvious market is small retailers and service establishments in neighborhood or central shopping districts. Don't overlook wholesale establishments, farms, mines, quarries, truckers, small manufacturers. Even a business with an in-house bookkeeper may want an outside firm to do more advanced work, and to check for errors, faulty technique—even dishonesty. Unfortunately, there are also businesses so small they cannot afford to pay you enough to keep their books.

If you are experienced in keeping books in a specialized trade or business, you may be able to find other clients limited to that trade or business and become bookkeeper for a group of firms. One bookkeeper worked for small grocers who were in a wholesaler's voluntary chain. He then charted a uniform classification of accounts, developed each grocer's operating ratios and the standard operating ratios for the whole group. This let him point out differences between each grocer's ratios and the standard ratios, then to analyze the differences to discover and correct bad practices. Standard operating ratios are available from Dun & Bradstreet Company and often from trade associations. The technique helped improve the efficiency of the whole group of retailers. It was a selling point for getting new grocery store clients. Another bookkeeping firm did the same for small laundries, and the same technique would apply to many kinds of business. As I will discuss in the marketing chapter, the point of advertising is to sell the benefits of the product or service, rather than the thing itself.

Even without prior experience in a trade or industry, anyone can pick out a likely one. Or you may have one client whose business has potential for developing into a specialty. There may be a concentration of similar businesses in your area, like restaurants, resort motels and campgrounds, contractors, or small manufacturers. Learn about the business and its problems. Talk to people in it. Contact the trade association and read trade journals.

Client services like these can be developed eventually, but in selling yourself and the business, your start-up market will be primarily individuals, including those with small businesses.

Bookkeeping and tax preparation are closely intertwined, and you should definitely be prepared to work both sides. A general practitioner needs to be versed in all the specialties of the business, including payroll, cost-accounting, and local, state, and federal taxes. Specialization can come later, after identifying an attractive market—what I call high-margin, low-volume clients. Some of these are profitable small businesses whose operations you become familiar with, and successful trade and professional people. Other specialties like serving senior citizens or people in agriculture may arise out of your geographic location. Some practices will probably already specialize in these markets, so try to think in terms of services that complement them. In agricultural areas think about shippers, produce brokers, warehouses and granaries, processors, farm equipment sales and repairs, pest control firms, scientific testing labs, auction barns, veterinarians, blacksmiths and welders, and agricultural supply houses. Industrial market areas may have engineering firms, testing labs, subcontractors, suppliers, shippers, and warehouses.

Franchises

The most visible and successful franchise in this business is H&R Block. Owning a Block franchise will all but guarantee a definable, predictable share of the market.

A franchise is not a *kind* of business but a way of conducting it by a continuous relationship between two business entities: the *franchisor*, which is selling the name and product or prepackaged services, and the *franchisee*, which buys them. As a licensing agreement, the franchise lets the franchisee sell the franchisor's products or services in a particular territory, under the agreement's terms and conditions.

Buying a franchise won't guarantee success, but some do have advantages. Better franchisors provide formal training programs, continuing management and technical guidance, standardized goods and services, sometimes a powerful brand name, and often a proven business format. A few franchisors—although I know of none in this business—offer financial assistance. Franchise buyers pay for the benefits, usually with an up-front franchise fee and continuing royalty payments.

The franchise relationship also has drawbacks. The initial fee is often high, royalty payments reduce profits, the franchisee's freedom of action is limited by the operating plan, and contract disputes are not uncommon. The decision to buy a franchise should never be made without a lot of research and, if necessary, the advice and assistance of experienced professionals.

I owned a franchise earlier in my career but decided after a few years that it was not for me. As with most ways of doing business it is an individual choice. You can scan the Appendix and take 'em or leave 'em.

Buying a Going Concern

You may solve some of the problems of building a clientele by buying an existing bookkeeping and tax-preparation service. If you do, be aware that this is a highly personalized business, and some clients will probably leave with the current owner. Be sure the price allows for the loss of those clients. If buying a going concern, you will need the advice of an experienced attorney, perhaps an experienced business broker, and an experienced escrow agent. Failure to use expert advice could be very costly.

If this appeals to you, here is a procedure that can help your search. Talk to people in the business to learn who is considering retirement. Consult trade sources, ads in trade publications, and even newspaper ads. When you find a business that looks promising make sure its specialties match your own. Then see why it is for sale. Inspect its financial records for the past three to five years to see if it is profitable. Check whether its fee structure is up to date. Note if its equipment is modern or needs to be replaced. Ask if good employees will stay with the business, and make sure you can assume the lease. Review the local government master plan for potential new competition, new housing, and zoning changes.

You have to do the same community survey as if you were setting up your own business, but also talk to the owners of competing businesses about the one you are considering buying. Find out from merchants and bankers in its market area whether it has loyal clients or if they have drifted away. Has it gone downhill, is it static, or growing?

If you decide to go ahead, you will be buying a number of tangible and intangible assets. Before setting a price to close the deal find out what those assets are worth. They usually include furniture, fixtures, equipment, and possibly the building. If it includes accounts receivable, study them very closely for their age and the larger accounts' credit standing. How successful was the previous owner in collecting from them? Is too much coming from accounts with slow payment histories? Does a lender have a security interest in the accounts receivable?

We've got so much taxation, I don't know of a single foreign product that enters this country untaxed except the answer to prayer.

—Mark Twain (1835-1910)
"New York Morals," speech, 1906

Check accounts payable and other liabilities for liens against the owner or the business. All states, the District of Columbia, and Virgin Islands have adopted the Uniform Commercial Code (UCC). The Code lets you file a Form UCC-3 with the Secretary of State for a name search to discover federal or state tax liens, attachment or judgment liens, and private encumbrances on the business's assets.

When you buy a business by purchasing corporate shares you get its assets along with its liabilities. When you buy a business's assets you usually do not buy its liabilities, but take care to check its outstanding debts. Court records will show if there are any liens against the business or any lawsuits pending; make sure you are not buying those, too. Check to see there will not be zoning changes, large businesses that may change the character of the neighborhood, a major competitor that will open its doors next to you, or code changes that will require a major upgrade of the premises. These are items you would determine in a community check anyway.

If the business rents its premises, make sure you can assume the lease or get a new one on favorable terms. Get a copy of any lease you will assume and review it carefully with an attorney. I don't know where they come from, but many commercial leases consist of dozens of pages of boilerplate in very muddy "legalese." A good lease can be essential to your business's success, so be sure its terms are understandable, unambiguous, and favorable.

If the company operates under a business name and the name is associated with a certain level of quality, you may want to buy the name. Whoever buys my business will have to use his own name, but I think that's how it ought to be. Sometimes, if you plan to replace an existing fictitious business name, you can try to negotiate a reduced sale price.

Most contracts for the sale of businesses include the seller's covenant not to compete within a given radius of the business for a certain number of years. Obviously, if the seller can hand over the keys then open up across the street on the following day, you won't be getting very much for your money.

Many sellers, particularly those who are retiring, may be willing to help run the business as consultants for a short time. When I retire I plan to stay on briefly to aid the transition to the new owner and incidentally make the purchase more attractive. Then I can also see whether or not to adjust the price for loss of a few clients. If you and your seller reach that understanding, you should spell it out in the sales contract as a consulting agreement. This arrangement can help smooth the transition or it can be a headache, depending on the parties. Think about it.

One nationwide franchise has a sale-of-business agreement tailored for bookkeeping services. Sale prices are typically based on 100 percent of gross income, paid off over five years. The actual price will depend on how many of the service's clients remain after the sale, and the annual payment is adjusted on that basis. On one hand, fewer clients are likely to depart when the seller stays on during the payoff period. This benefits both buyer and seller. On the other hand, some sellers refuse to let go and may become a daily fixture. It can mean an intolerable level of interference in the business's day-to-day operation and greater difficulty to establish your own identity. So try to limit the seller's presence to an occasional consultation.

Also, if the businesses's employees are an asset to the business, they should be told about the sale and assured that they will have a job with you.

One contract protection for the buyer is a set of seller warranties, with the buyer's right to deduct from the sale price the cost of any undisclosed debts or the value of any divergence from the warranties. Some breaches may let you cancel the deal. The seller usually warrants good title to real and personal property, the disclosure of all material facts, the truth and accuracy of financial statements, that all liabilities are disclosed in the balance sheet, and that there is no litigation or governmental proceeding against the business.

All this distasteful stuff was dreamed up by lawyers, who are notorious deal breakers. You will have to get a sense of whom you are dealing with and how much assurance you need when you purchase the business. Know what you want, use your own judgment, and keep control of the negotiations and decision-making power. Listen to your attorney—that is what you hired him for—but don't forget you are in charge. Your lawyer is not going to buy and run the business.

There's more. You need to make sure all applicable taxes, including withholding, income, and unemployment have been paid. Clearance certificates from the appropriate government agencies will cover them. Also notify the IRS of the sale, and be sure local taxes have been paid.

It will probably cost more to buy an existing business than to start from scratch on your own, but you could be up and running right away. If you need a bank loan to help buy the business, you want one big enough leave sufficient capital of your own to carry you to break-even, but not so big that you can't cover the payments. The seller may be willing to carry back financing for purchase of the business. The same rule about manageable debt applies, but also try to get an option to purchase your own note in case the seller decides to discount and sell it later on.

Added start-up expenses may include costs of repair, renovation, new equipment, and possible health or building code upgrades. Finally, a bank will probably require additional security for any loan.

Purchasing a business takes a lot of work and study. You should proceed with professional help. I recommend reading *The Complete Guide to Buying and Selling a Business*, by Arnold S. Goldstein. You probably won't end up doing it yourself, but you will be a better client for a business broker or lawyer who handles the deal.

Drive-by and walk-by traffic are unimportant. You want referral business. You can be in a good office building on the 17th floor. Your clients won't care; it doesn't matter.

6

Office Space

YOUR office space needs will depend on whether you do a part-time start-up or launch a full-blown assault. This short chapter can do no more than introduce the very important question of how easily your customers will find their way to your door and what they will encounter when they get there. It is an important subject; don't be misled by the chapter's brevity.

Home Office or Commercial Office?

We live in the age where it is very chic to work out of your home. This is probably best for the part-time practitioner. Part time or not, it has advantages and disadvantages. The first advantage is that your office is at home. You already own or rent it, so there is no additional outlay to get an office or commute to work. There is, however, a reduction in living space and convenience even if the home has a spare room.

The first disadvantage is that the business is at home. In my opinion a single room is not adequate to operate this kind of business. You need to maintain client confidentiality, and that means an area that provides privacy. If you have commercial space, there must be some place for the clients to wait. You need another place to interview clients with the door closed.

The typical bookkeeping office breaks down into five spaces, although some spaces can share the same room. The first is a reception and secretarial area. In the home office, obviously, it will be only a reception area. There should be a couch, chairs, lamps, tables, art, and plants to create a comfortable setting. In a commercial office it might also have an assistant-receptionist's desk, chair, typewriter or computer, telephone, lamps, and filing cabinet. Second, a records and filing area is essential. If space is tight, portable filing cabinets instead of a storage room will suffice. Third, there should be a data-processing area, which in a small office would be combined with the write-up area. A larger firm might have (fourth) a separate write-up area for an assistant. Each such area would have a desk or table with chair, lamp, and calculator or computer, and possibly file cabinets and storage. It could also hold a sizable library, although that's less likely today. Fifth, is your office. Since this is where you meet clients, it should have a good quality desk and chair, client chairs, lamps, a filing cabinet, bookshelves for your library and the like, and whatever personal effects you feel enhance the identity you want to project. The minimum you can get away with is two rooms. On the facing page is a rough sketch of my office and how I furnish and equip the essential areas in it.

If you are at home and want to create an environment in which people can wait while you are dealing with a client in private, you need another part of the house where those clients can wait. They don't always arrive on time for their appointments; some are early birds, others are habitually tardy, a few walk in unannounced, and many overstay their appointments.

The other issue unfavorable to the home office is location. You couldn't operate the business out of the home effectively if you lived out on a ranch and all your clients were in town. That is an extreme example to illustrate a point. You need a central business location for a business, and few homes have that. In fact, what makes home desirable as a home is its lack of a central location. It is a major reason for zoning laws. And it brings up the final disadvantage, which is that a home should be a sanctuary away from the rest of the world, providing a clear separation between your personal and professional lives. Working at home may affect how clients perceive the business, too, especially if they have to wait in the living room with toys on the floor, the kids watching cartoons on television, pets wandering around, and other family activities going on.

Your family can be resentful of the business's intrusion on home life, and it can intrude on your own home life as well. Inevitably, there will be a problem juggling time when neighbors or friends visit. Another reason why I am unexcited about using the home for an office is you need to consider whether or not you have the self-discipline to work at home. I tried it and I can't. I don't want to try it again.

Now that I've made myself out to be a hard-hearted ogre, driving capable and talented people out of their homes into the harsh commercial real estate market, I will admit that the disadvantages of a home office can be overcome. Many successful practitioners operate bookkeeping practices from home offices. But they do it by recognizing the problems and taking care of them. My own hunch—although one I have not researched—is that a good home-based bookkeeper could increase his or her income much above the costs involved by moving to a good business location and hiring a trained support staff. If I haven't convinced you, and you want to work out of the home anyway, then a good guide for setting up at home is Linda Stern's *Bookkeeping on Your Home-Based PC*, published in 1993 by McGraw-Hill. It covers a lot of software

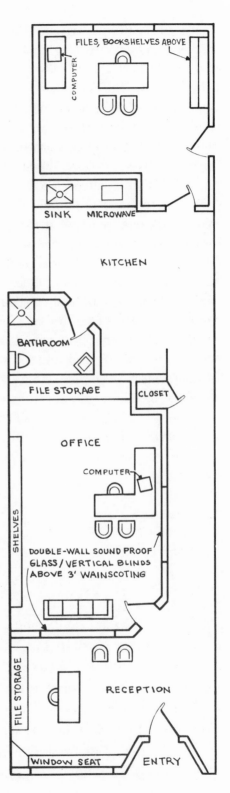

that for the most part is out of date, but it is based on interviews with bookkeepers who work at home.

Shopping for Space

Finding an office in a good business location is not difficult and need not be prohibitively expensive. A bookkeeper and tax preparer can prosper in a modest space in an office building. In most cities that is a buyer's market. You don't need a storefront location. I happen to have an office with a storefront location, but I have always thought of it as office space, not a storefront. There aren't many office buildings in my town. In a rural setting it is nice to have a visual presence on the main street, close to the center of town. It is also gratifying to have a sign out on the street with your name on it. But drive-by and walk-by traffic are unimportant. You want people to come to you by referral. If you live in an urban area you can be in a good office building up on the 17th floor. Your clients won't care. It doesn't matter.

The public's image of your space does matter. It should project a clean, safe, well-lighted professional setting. The rest is personal and should reflect your personality, your plans for the business, and its potential needs for growth. If the office is at home, the ideal would be to have a separate entrance, an anteroom to wait in, and no homey clutter to distract you and your client from business. A converted garage or guest house—even a basement or attic—might serve that purpose adequately.

Next Two Pages:

The first short form 1040A appeared in 1917 for individuals with income of $3,000 or less. Until then, income classes below $3,000 paid no income tax. In 1941 Form 1040, which had reached four pages in 1937, was restructured to permit removal of pages 3 and 4, dealing with capital gains, business income, and income from trusts, estates, and depreciation.

For tax year 1943 both the 1040A (shown here) and 1040 were redesigned to add a "Victory Tax" and to add for the first time a "refund or credit due" space necessitated by the introduction of tax withholding on wages

FORM 1040 A
Treasury Dept., Internal Revenue Service

OPTIONAL U. S. INDIVIDUAL INCOME AND VICTORY TAX RETURN · CALENDAR YEAR 1943

[This form *may* be used instead of Form 1040 if gross income is not more than $3,000 and is *only* from the sources stated in items 1 and 2 below.]

Do not write in these spaces
Serial No.
Amount paid, $
(Cashier's stamp)

NAME _____
Please print. If this return is for a husband and wife, use both first names.

ADDRESS _____
Print street and number or rural route — City or town — State

OCCUPATION _____
Social Security No. (if any) _____

Cash—Check—M. O.

Your Income

1. Enter the TOTAL amount, before deductions for taxes, dues, insurance, bonds, etc., that you received in 1943 as salary, wages, bonuses, commissions, etc. (Members of armed forces read instruction 6)

List Employer's Name	City and State	Amount
		$
	Total	

2. Enter here any amounts you received in 1943 in dividends, interest, and annuities..........

3. Now add items 1 and 2 to get your TOTAL INCOME and enter it here..........

Your Credit for Dependents

4. List the persons—other than wife or husband—who on July 1, 1943, obtained their *chief support from you* if they were not yet 18, or were mentally or physically unable to support themselves.

Name of Dependent	Relationship	If 18 years or over, give reason for listing

You are allowed a credit of $385 for each dependent. However, if you are not a married person living with wife or husband, you may nevertheless be the head of a family as defined in No. 6 on the other side of the form. If you are the head of a family *only because of the dependents you listed above*, allow $385 for each listed dependent *except one*.
Enter total dependency credit here..........

5. Subtract item 4 from item 3. Enter the difference here. (Enter item 3 if item 4 is blank)

Your Tax Bill and Forgiveness

6. Turn over this form and check the box at the top which applies to you. Then, using the figure you entered in item 5, find your income tax in the table. Enter the amount here..........

7. In the space on the back of this form, figure your Victory tax on item 3. Enter the tax here.....

8. Now add items 6 and 7. Enter the total here..........

9. If you filed a tax return on 1942 income, enter the amount of tax here. However, before entering anything, read *carefully* instruction 4..........

10. Enter item 8 or item 9, whichever is larger..........

11. FORGIVENESS FEATURE: *Don't fill in A, B, and C below if either item 8 or 9 is $50 or less.*

  A Enter item 8 or 9, whichever is smaller..........
  B Take three-fourths of A above. Enter this amount or $50, whichever is larger. This is the *forgiven* part of the tax..........
  C Subtract B from A. This is the *unforgiven* part of the tax. Enter it here....

12. Add item 10 to the amount in item 11C, if any. Enter the total here. This is your total income and Victory tax..........

What You've Paid and What You Owe

13.   A Enter here your income and Victory taxes withheld by your employer....
  B Enter here the total sums you paid last year on your 1942 income tax bill
  C Enter here any 1943 income tax payments last September and December..
  D Now add the figures in A, B and C and enter the total here..........

14. If the tax in item 12 is more than the total payments in item 13, you owe the difference. Enter it here. If the payments are greater, write "NONE" and skip items 15 and 16......

Terms of Payment or Refund

15. You may postpone, until not later than March 15, 1945, payment of the amount you owe up to one half of item 11C. Enter the postponed amount here..........

16. Enter the amount you are paying with this return (subtract item 15 from item 14)..........

17. If the TOTAL of your 1943 payments (item 13) is larger than your tax (item 12), enter the difference. You have overpaid your 1943 tax by this amount..........
Check (✔) what you want done: Refund it to me ☐ Credit it on my 1944 estimated tax ☐

I declare under the penalties of perjury that this return has been examined by me, and to the best of my knowledge and belief, is a true, correct and complete return.

Date_____,1944 (Signature)_____ (Signature)_____
(If this return includes income of both a husband and wife, it must be signed by both)

1. Single (and not head of family) on July 1, 1943 . . . . . □   **A**

2. Married but not living with wife or husband (and not head of family) on July 1, 1943 . . . . □

If you checked No. 1 or No. 2 above, find your tax in column **A** of the table below

3. Married and living with wife or husband on July 1, 1943, but each filing separate returns on this form . . . . □   **B**

If you checked No. 3 above, find your tax in column **B** of the table below

4. Married and living with wife or husband on July 1, 1943, and only one had gross income during the year . . . . □

5. Married and living with wife or husband on July 1, 1943, and this return includes gross income of both wife and husband for the entire year . . . . □   **C**

6. Others who are head of family (a single person or married person not living with wife and husband who exercises family control and supports closely connected dependent relative(s) in one household) on July 1, 1943 . . . . □

   (State number of such dependent relatives _____)

If you checked No. 4, 5, or 6 above, find your tax in column **C** of the table below

Now read down to where the figure you entered in item 5 falls, and then across to your column. Enter the tax you find there as item 6 on the other side.

If Income subject to tax (item 5 on other side) is OVER	But not over	COLUMN A Your TAX is	COLUMN B Your TAX is	COLUMN C Your TAX is	If Income subject to tax (item 5 on other side) is OVER	But not over	COLUMN A Your TAX is	COLUMN B Your TAX is	COLUMN C Your TAX is	If Income subject to tax (item 5 on other side) is OVER	But not over	COLUMN A Your TAX is	COLUMN B Your TAX is	COLUMN C Your TAX is
$0	$525	$0	$0	$0	$1,350	$1,375	$141	$122	$10	$2,175	$2,200	$283	$264	$150
525	550	1	0	0	1,375	1,400	145	126	14	2,200	2,225	288	269	155
550	575	4	0	0	1,400	1,425	149	130	17	2,225	2,250	292	273	159
575	600	7	0	0	1,425	1,450	154	135	21	2,250	2,275	296	277	163
600	625	11	0	0	1,450	1,475	158	139	25	2,275	2,300	301	282	168
625	650	15	0	0	1,475	1,500	162	143	29	2,300	2,325	305	286	172
650	675	20	3	0	1,500	1,525	167	148	34	2,325	2,350	309	290	176
675	700	24	6	0	1,525	1,550	171	152	38	2,350	2,375	314	295	181
700	725	28	9	0	1,550	1,575	175	156	42	2,375	2,400	318	299	185
725	750	33	14	0	1,575	1,600	180	161	47	2,400	2,425	322	303	189
750	775	37	18	0	1,600	1,625	184	165	51	2,425	2,450	327	308	194
775	800	41	22	0	1,625	1,650	188	169	55	2,450	2,475	331	312	198
800	825	46	27	0	1,650	1,675	193	174	60	2,475	2,500	335	316	202
825	850	50	31	0	1,675	1,700	197	178	64	2,500	2,525	340	321	207
850	875	54	35	0	1,700	1,725	201	182	68	2,525	2,550	344	325	211
875	900	59	40	0	1,725	1,750	206	187	73	2,550	2,575	348	329	215
900	925	63	44	0	1,750	1,775	210	191	77	2,575	2,600	353	334	220
925	950	67	48	0	1,775	1,800	214	195	81	2,600	2,625	357	338	224
950	975	71	52	0	1,800	1,825	218	199	85	2,625	2,650	361	342	228
975	1,000	76	57	0	1,825	1,850	223	204	90	2,650	2,675	366	347	233
1,000	1,025	80	61	0	1,850	1,875	227	208	94	2,675	2,700	371	351	237
1,025	1,050	84	65	0	1,875	1,900	231	212	98	2,700	2,725	376	355	241
1,050	1,075	89	70	0	1,900	1,925	236	217	103	2,725	2,750	381	359	245
1,075	1,100	93	74	0	1,925	1,950	240	221	107	2,750	2,775	386	364	250
1,100	1,125	97	78	0	1,950	1,975	244	225	111	2,775	2,800	391	369	254
1,125	1,150	102	83	0	1,975	2,000	249	230	116	2,800	2,825	396	374	258
1,150	1,175	106	87	0	2,000	2,025	253	234	120	2,825	2,850	401	379	263
1,175	1,200	110	91	0	2,025	2,050	257	238	124	2,850	2,875	406	384	267
1,200	1,225	115	96	0	2,050	2,075	262	243	129	2,875	2,900	411	389	271
1,225	1,250	119	100	0	2,075	2,100	266	247	133	2,900	2,925	416	394	276
1,250	1,275	123	104	0	2,100	2,125	270	251	137	2,925	2,950	421	399	280
1,275	1,300	128	109	1	2,125	2,150	275	256	142	2,950	2,975	426	404	284
1,300	1,325	132	113	4	2,150	2,175	279	260	146	2,975	3,000	431	409	289
1,325	1,350	136	117	7										

Figure Your Victory Tax In This Space

a) Copy here the figure you entered in item 3 on the other side of this form . . . . $

b) If you checked No. 1, 2, 3, 4 or 6 at the top of this page, enter $624, *or*
If you checked No. 5, and both you and your wife or husband each had income of more than $624, enter $1248 here; however, if either of you had $624 or less, add the smaller of the two incomes to $624 and enter the total here. The figure you enter is your Victory tax exemption . . . . $

c) Now subtract the amount in line b from the amount in line a. Enter the difference here . . . . $

d) You now figure your net Victory tax. In the table below first find the percentage which applies to you and circle it. Now, multiply the amount you entered in line c by the rate you circled. Enter the result here and in item 7 on the other side. (See examples below.) This method automatically allows you your credit, which depends on whether you are married or single and how many dependents you have . . . .

DEPENDENTS	None		2	3	4	5	6	7	8	9	10
Single	3.75%	3.65%	3.55%	3.45%	3.35%	3.25%	3.15%	3.05%	2.95%	2.85%	2.75%
Married	3.0%	2.9%	2.8%	2.7%	2.6%	2.5%	2.4%	2.3%	2.2%	2.1%	2.0%

Those who checked No. 6 at the top of this page should use the rates for married persons in the table just above. However, count as dependents only the number for whom you claimed credit in item 4 on the other side of this form.

EXAMPLE 1 — Single, no dependents

Amount entered in line c	$1525
Net Victory Tax rate	× .0375
(from table above)	7625
	10675
	4575
	$57.1875
Net Victory Tax (enter in line d)	$57.19

EXAMPLE 2 — Married, no dependents

Amount entered in line c	$1525
Net Victory Tax rate	× .03
(from table above)	$45.75
Net Victory Tax (enter in line d)	$45.75

EXAMPLE 3 — Married, 2 dependents

Amount entered in line c	$1525
Net Victory Tax rate	× .028
(from table above)	12200
	3050
	$42.700
Net Victory Tax (enter in line d)	$42.70

The costs of commercial space are dictated by geography. Your task is to look around for attractive, well located, affordable space. People in urban areas have a special option. There are entities in most big and middle-sized cities that lease large blocks of office buildings and sublet them as executive suites. These suites provide full time reception areas, support services, shared office machines, maintenance and janitorial services, and a nicely appointed office setting for a single monthly fee. It is not the cheapest way to go, but it addresses a lot of problems the beginner has to face. Otherwise, finding good office space is a matter of taking the best you can afford. Another possibility is to rent space, preferably a separate office or suite, from an established practitioner. It will be in a location people associate with the business and may provide you with some overflow clients.

Get It in Writing

Wherever you rent, get a written lease or rental agreement. At a minimum, a rental document will exactly describe the property, and state the rental amount and when to pay it. Usually it also spells out which are your responsibilities and which are the landlord's. Some rents cover all utilities and janitorial services; others pay only for space, with everything else extra. The rental document should also state who is responsible for the improvements and how to allocate insurance and liability for the premises. Sublease rights, if any, may help you defray rental costs while you are there or recoup some costs if you need to close shop and vacate. Compare the terms of rentals before selecting one and be sure you are comparing apples with apples before you decide where to set up.

A "rental agreement" usually refers to a month-to-month arrangement. Either party can terminate it at any time after giving proper statutory notice, and the landlord can usually modify its terms, including the rent, in the same way. A "lease" covers a longer period of time, usually a year, and all the terms are fixed for that period, but you are committed to paying the rent and meeting other obligations for the lease's term. The method of terminating is spelled out in the lease. There are advantages to leases and rental agreements. Weigh each carefully before deciding which to seek. If the rental market suggests you won't have any rent increases in the next few months, a month-to-month agreement will give you more flexibility than a lease. If rents are notching up and you are certain of staying put, you would want at least a year's lease, but a way to get out from under it if things go badly.

I said this earlier but, at the risk of being redundant, I must caution readers to *understand* what the lease says. All of it. Don't become over-awed by legalistic jargon. You want clear, unambiguous lease terms that you can live with and thrive on.

Buying Your Office

The real estate market may justify purchasing office space. This will be especially true if property values are rising, if you can afford to buy, and if the property is a promising investment. If you decide to consider purchasing office space, shop first for the best commercial real estate agent in the area. Shopping for real estate agents, as with all specialists, means getting references and questioning them about the agent's abilities and past performance.

If you have the capital and want the responsibility, buying will put you ahead in the long run if the business prospers. You won't face rent increases. Your building can be security for a later loan and it is a store of wealth as you build equity in it. Naturally, your cash situation will determine whether you buy or rent. If buying is a possibility, consider acquisition techniques like seller financing, lease options, and leasing part of your building to help pay it off.

As with all enterprises, you must position your business to serve a particular niche, then establish and maintain it with the tools of marketing: advertising, publicity, and public relations.

7

Marketing Your Services

THE cornerstone of successful entrepreneurship is to find and keep customers or clients who will pay for your product or services. You won't have a bookkeeping and tax-preparation business without clients, and you won't get them if nobody knows about you and your services. It may surprise you to learn that once in business you will set about selling those services as hard as you do the work and manage the business. You will do this selling much of the time without even noticing. It is better if you know that you are doing it, so you can organize and focus your efforts to greatest effect. It is much better if you think about how you will organize and focus your efforts before you even open the doors.

Mysteries of Marketing

This organizing and focusing is called marketing, and to do it well you need a marketing plan and a commitment to follow through on it every day of your working life. Marketing is more complex than buying advertising, getting publicity, and building public relations. Those are all part of marketing. Marketing itself involves learning and staying aware of potential clients' tastes, wants, and even spending patterns, then responding to them. It begins with the research you did to choose a market, it concentrates on the clients you want in that market, and it changes as their needs change.

Your potential clients will be primarily businesses and individuals who have never had a bookkeeper or tax preparer. Established services' clients ordinarily leave for only three reasons: (1) The practitioner—having died, retired, or moved away—is no longer available; (2) the practitioner—for legal, ethical, or moral reasons—has advised against a course the client insists on taking, and the client wants one who will do as told; or (3) the client is shopping for cheaper service. Very occasionally a client, feeling neglected or charged for services not rendered, will look elsewhere. If the service works to maintain good client relations, that won't happen often. But, except for neglected clients and those whose practitioner is gone, you probably won't want the business that defecting clients have to offer.

That is why your new bookkeeping and tax-preparation service must use every marketing tool there is to find *new* clients. To compound the problem, new business-start-up clients may be on shaky ground and if they fail they won't be clients for very long. What you face, in any case, is six months or a year to break-even, then a long pull to build a comfortable practice. That isn't the cheeriest news but that's how it is. If you feel discouraged, just remember that everyone started out this way. You will just have to conserve your resources and work to get those clients. As with all enterprises, you must position your bookkeeping/tax-preparation business to serve a particular niche in the market then establish and maintain its position with the tools of marketing: advertising, publicity, and public relations. You have to work hardest at it when starting out, but then you will have more time in which to do it.

Publicity

Rather than discuss advertising first, let's start with publicity, which is simply public recognition of you and your business. You are going to create and get publicity whether or not or you advertise. Publicity is simple. It begins with the business's appearance and character. As long as you are in business, you get publicity. When the client first sees your front door that is publicity. If you have a street-front location like mine, the office façade and sign make the first impression. You want the impression to be favorable. If it is, you may get the client to see the inside of your office, where you don't want any dust, stale air, gloom, or untidiness. I prefer to think of these impressions not as an image but part of your identity. Image sounds like an illusion, all smoke and mirrors. You want everything to be genuine. The client sees you next, and you definitely want to look every inch the professional. I don't mean that you should always wear formal business attire. In our town that seems a little stuffy, and few professionals here wear neckties or the feminine equivalent, at least not all the time. But you should be well groomed and look ready to put in a hard day's work on your client's affairs.

Right behind identity—and towering over it—comes reputation. Reputation in a small bookkeeping and tax-preparation business is everything. This is especially true in a rural location like mine, but it is just as important even in large "anonymous" cities, where competition may be fiercer and word eventually gets around. When selling your services, *you* are what is being sold. Frequently how people perceive you as a person will matter more than the product line you may be introducing to them. You need to be sure each client knows you for the honest, dependable person you are. This means not only promoting your strengths and knowledge but also admitting your weaknesses and limitations.

A well-organized, presentable work space and your professional appearance also support the confidence that you must have and project to the client. Unless you believe in yourself and let the client know it by your words, actions, and surroundings, you will have a hard time selling your wares. On the other hand, if you present yourself in a confident, professional manner, people will expect you to charge the professional rate that your services deserve. This is all part of aiming for the middle to upper segment of the market and avoiding that troublesome low end. You do that in part by identifying your clients, but next you must arrange all your business activities, beginning with these basic steps, to work for and acquire just those clients.

Further, even though you may have to be a generalist starting out, you should encourage a public perception of you as specialist as soon as possible. If, for example, you cultivate a referral network among lawyers as a specialist in estate planning or money management, they will associate your name with that specialty and get to know you as, say, Pat Moore the Retirement Expert, or Chris Reid the Estate Planner or Sandy Wilson the Tax Wizard, and so on. These tags will help attract clients interested in that kind of service, and you can more easily discern whether the client will benefit from other services you offer or want to offer. In other words, start to shape your practice right away.

Whether you have reached the point of settling on a specialty or not, it also helps to introduce yourself as soon as possible to other practitioners in the area. Some might want to contract out or refer business to you during the busy season if not more often. Whatever the meeting's result, getting to know others in the business is invariably good for all concerned.

Publicity becomes more familiar when we think of promotional activities like giving seminars and getting them noticed in the local newspaper's *Upcoming Events* or *Community Calendar* section. This is really the second level and is just as important as laying the groundwork. To do it well, learn the media in your area and think about publicity-generating events appropriate to the right medium or media. You don't have to get established before you start using the media. You will have lots of free time when starting out to think of new ideas and new combinations of services to offer. Then arrange to tell people about them in seminars, lectures, and meetings of civic groups—or teach a class.

What if you announce a seminar and nobody comes? It doesn't matter. The secret of marketing is to keep at it and to get your name where people see it. Eventually, people will notice. There is nothing like repetition to lend weight and authority to your name. If you can't think of a new subject to speak on, re-title the old one; shift its emphasis. Keep up with new developments and regulations. Stake out your specialty. Be the expert. Contact special organizations in your area and offer to discuss a topic of interest to them like tax-saving advice, or estate or retirement planning. People will start to come to your seminars. Then you can project your air of knowledge, your caring personality, and your sterling integrity. Finally, the clients you want will begin to walk through your front door.

Think of publicity as event-oriented and, once you have familiarized yourself with the media in your area, send your local *Business Beat* editor notices not only of seminars and lectures but of bringing new staff members and assistants into the firm, acquiring new professional designations, winning awards, completing courses of study. You won't get plugs every time you send in a notice, but a concise note of your activities sent to the right department will be published occasionally. You don't have to be a writer. You want just the facts. Keep it brief and tell who did what, when, where, why, and how. Use an "inverted pyramid" style with the most important items first and minor ones trailing after them. Some newspapers have a "how to" packet for submitting information. If you follow the rules, you get more in print.

Getting publicity takes a lot of effort. It is cheaper than advertising, and it pays off when you get it. Some of the best publicity for any business is word-of-mouth. You can't buy it, and it gives a better result than any form of advertising. Remember however, that word-of-mouth depends absolutely on you and the quality of your work.

Advertising

Even though you may be able to do well on publicity alone, successful advertising will keep your name before the public and remind it of the services you offer. Advertising does that better than all your efforts at getting publicity and it can be managed economically and productively.

The first rule of advertising is to sell the benefits rather than your name or even the product. Madison Avenue used to call this "selling the sizzle instead of the steak." The last time you bought a product from an ad, you expected it to enhance your life just as the ad promised. The product was simply the means to that end, and, if it worked as promised, you enjoyed the benefits every time you used it. Similarly, the last time you used the Yellow Pages you had a problem and that is where you went to find a solution. Always think of the benefits you are selling. Present them in the clearest, most definite, and concise manner you can, and your advertisements will work for you.

Copy writing and design are very specialized skills, and you may want to consult a specialist to write and design your advertising. Successful advertising people warn that if you draft important ads yourself they will probably look like everyone else's and get lost in the crowd. Consider whether your message is important enough to get professional assistance. If you hire an ad agency, shop around as you would for any service. Ask to see their portfolios and look for ads that have been around long enough to look familiar. The older they are, the better. One way to keep expenses down for professional assistance might be to have an agency sell you the design and idea, then to have it executed by a good but cheaper graphic artist.

Whether you decide to handle your own advertising or let an expert do it, get all the ideas you can from existing ads. Read old newspapers and periodicals. If some of the old ads are still being used, it is probably because they work. Try to see what makes them work and imitate them. This is a case where nothing succeeds like success.

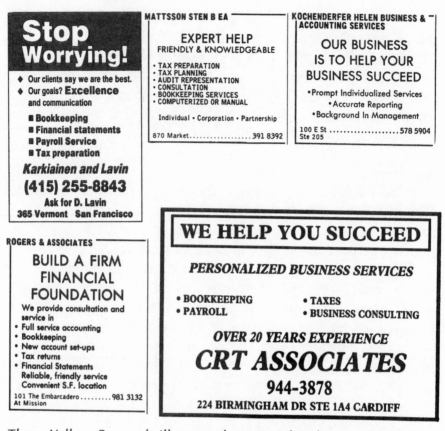

These Yellow Page ads illustrate the principles discussed below.

Any advertising you use should promote name recognition by repetition. That means that you won't begin to see results until your message has been around awhile and begun to sink into public awareness. In the same way, any print material you hand out, any brochures, promotions, or newsletters you mail out, any printed materials with your name or the company's name on it should be identified by consistency in its name, typography, and any logo to help fix it in people's minds.

You have to advertise. There is no other way to get some messages across to your market. Don't try to make publicity do the work of advertising, or vice versa. If you want to try a different kind of advertising, go ahead and experiment but test every ad for pull. Be sure to ask new clients how they learned about the business or decided to give you a call. This way you can track the return on your promotional dollar and spend where it is most effective.

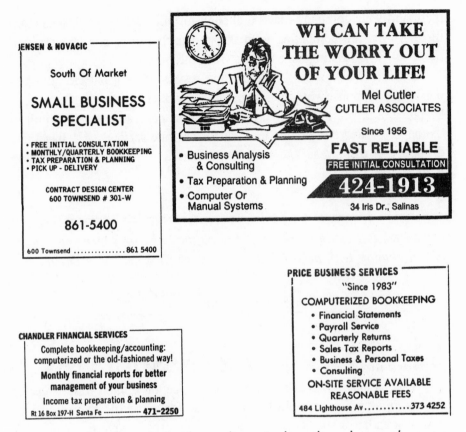

Whether a display ad or a few column inches, the rules are the same.

Yellow Pages

For most small businesses a Yellow Page ad is essential. It should be drafted to present your name or the business's and the services provided. A common mistake I see in bookkeeping and tax preparation advertising is to promote the name rather than benefits of the services offered. The ad must emphasize bookkeeping, tax preparation, financial planning, insurance service, stock brokering, or whatever combination of specialties is offered. If you have acquired credentials or special accreditation, that should also be prominently mentioned. Remember to stress the benefits. Your name and the company name can take a subsidiary position.

Yellow Page ads in telephone books are usually designed by telephone company representatives. If you are not satisfied with the ad they suggest, it may be worth finding an advertising agency to create one for you. Starting out, you probably don't need a quarter-page display ad. If your services are sufficiently specialized, a few column inches describing them and your company may be enough to pull in the clients who want them. If you are competing with companies that offer similar services, try to tell what distinguishes yours from the others.

As with all advertising, evaluate the results of Yellow-Page advertising by the response you get. In my area it works very well. One bookkeeper in a large city reported that his yellow page ad seemed to pull in "shoppers," low-end clients looking for cut-rate services. He has since dropped his display ad and relies on referrals for business. Everything is local.

Commerce is generally understood to be the basis on which the power of this country hath been raised, and on which it must ever stand.

—Benjamin Franklin (1706-1790)

Press and Air Waves

I have found newspaper advertising to be of limited value, useful mainly to advertise an event like a seminar for a specific market group. If your area has a special publication for that group, advertise there, not in the general daily or weekly newspaper. Timing is important, too. Advertising tax-preparer services during tax season might help, but there would be very little return from keeping ads running year around in a newspaper.

With the advent of cable, television ads are very reasonably priced. Most cable providers can generate and repeat a good, high-quality television ad for a very reasonable cost. Usually you can customize the ad to promote a seminar or special event relating to your practice.

Direct Mail

Direct mail advertising is useful to offer specific services or products to targeted clients. It can be a fairly effective way to generate new business. The problem, as we all know, is that people receive tons of junk mail, and the slicker it is, the more likely people are to toss your message without opening it.

If you do decide to do a mailing, hand-address the envelopes. This is most practical when you have only a hundred or so, not a few thousand, to send out. But if you or perhaps you and a secretary or part-time help can address 10 or 20 envelopes a day, the job is manageable. The better the mailing list is, the better the result. Your own client list is the best source. Purchased mailing lists usually get percentage returns in the low single digits.

You need to use the personal touch to follow up on any mass mailing. Keep a tickler file keyed to when you mailed the materials. After the mailing has gone out telephone the client with a reminder of what you sent: "By the way, did you get that piece I sent you?" or "I thought of you when I was reviewing that material, so I sent it to you," and "Is it something you would be interested in?" My experience is that a mailer is not much use unless it is directed personally to each individual client and followed up by either a telephone call or other personal contact.

Miscellaneous Media

I find that ads like your name on menus or telephone jackets, are rarely a good investment. It does get the business name before the public, but I have never had anyone come in and say, "Hey, I came to see you because I saw your name on the menu in a restaurant." It doesn't seem to work that way.

In some areas it helps to participate in a Welcome Wagon program by providing rebate coupons for your services to newcomers. Some advertising, like sponsoring Little League teams, has a public relations benefit. Because your advertising will be on the back of uniforms, the kids' parents and others in the community will appreciate your support, and it could lead to additional business. I also think that kind of advertising is more effective than a passive sort of flyer or other print medium.

Public Relations

Simply stated, public relations involves getting to be known in association with the right things. Joining and participating in service clubs is a good way to make contacts and network. It is also a way to be known as someone who is interested in more than making a buck. I belong to the Kiwanis Club in my town and find it not only enjoyable but also an excellent way to establish myself in the community. I also serve on the board of directors of two or three small nonprofit organizations like Big Brothers/Big Sisters. It is to anyone's advantage to volunteer time to help other people through a local or nationally recognized charitable organization.

Joining means above all to give community service. It is not a direct solicitation for business and it would be a mistake to join with that in mind. It does get you out in the community meeting people and making yourself known. Becoming an involved and concerned member of your community is something you should do because your success depends ultimately upon the welfare of the community. Just incidentally people will know who you are and that you are concerned, and they are likelier to think of you favorably when they need the services you offer.

On another level, good public relations involves everything you do. It requires empathizing with others and acting on the feeling without considering it a chore or expecting a return. It shows up as: being honest in advertising; dealing fairly with clients, creditors, and employees; admitting mistakes and compensating for them; answering mail and telephone calls promptly; paying bills on time; and helping people when they need it. As Mark Twain said, "Always do right. It will gratify some people and astonish the rest." You can't have better press than that.

Magic Marketing Books

Finally, you are not alone. A number of books have recognized and addressed small-business people's needs for establishing and promoting their livelihoods. I have listed a handful in the Appendix, but a few deserve mention here. Foremost are Jay Levinson's *Guerrilla Marketing* series. Don't let his paramilitary titles put you off. Levinson is a former vice president and creative director of two the country's biggest advertising agencies, and a marketing consultant to Fortune 500 firms as well as small businesses. His growing collection of books will demystify marketing like nothing else in print.

Two more worthy titles are Bart Brodsky and Janet Geis's *Finding Your Niche—Marketing Your Professional Service,* and Marilyn and Tom Ross's *Big Marketing Ideas for Small Service Businesses*. The authors of each book are marketing specialists who also teach and write on the subject. They tell how a marketing plan can attract good clients and assure their continued satisfaction.

*If you always do a little more
than the job seems to call
for, it is very hard for the
client to find service better
than yours anywhere else.*

8

Client Relations

ONCE you define your client base and attract new clients to the business, be prepared to give all the service you promised—and more. No matter how good a marketing campaign you have, it is of little use if you don't follow up with the best efforts you can muster. That is the only way to satisfy and keep clients. Satisfied clients are the key to whether your business flourishes or founders; for, without clients you have no business.

Client satisfaction depends on what my father used to call "giving 110 percent." If you always do a little more than the job seems to call for, it is very hard for the client to find service better than yours anywhere else. Also, if people feel they are getting value for their money, they will often overlook occasional lapses and imperfections like failing to be invariably on time, permitting a typo to slip by, or making an arithmetic mistake—which happens, Lord knows, even in this age of computers. Further, if they know you are doing the best job you can, and it is a better job than they can get anywhere else, they are even likelier to be understanding when you get yourself in a jam. (And—welcome to the real world—you will get in jams.)

Off to a Good Start

Good client relations have to begin well. That is, they start with the initial interview. This interview, running anywhere from a half-hour to an hour depending on the job's complexity, has to be free—no charge. There is no business relationship yet. The potential client is just shopping, and you are still just marketing your wares. What you are selling is your services, which depend heavily on client confidence. The best thing you can do to help generate that confidence is to learn to *listen*. Talking to clients is secondary and serves a limited function.

The reason why you talk to a client, at least in the initial interview, is to learn what the client perceives to be his or her needs with respect to your services. You have to let the client lead the conversation. Bide your time. Try to steer the conversation toward the areas you know are critical for the information you need by asking questions while you listen. Listening is not easy, and few of us are good natural listeners. A psychologist might explain our tendency to deaf ears in terms of "closure." We all want to make sense of our perceptions as soon as possible, and most of us will leap to the easiest conclusion to do it. Those first few facts can never reveal enough, however, so wait to hear everything from the client so that you don't end up way out in left field—or out of the ball park. That is why the client should lead. Listen and ask questions only to elicit more facts. Ask the same question in different ways several times throughout the interview, if necessary, to get them straight. Try to link the facts loosely and keep them loose until there is only one way to read them. Take notes if you must, but keep them brief.

Then, once the client seems to have said everything, try to capsulize and play it back to be sure that you heard right. If you did, then give a brief outline of how you can address the issues with specific services to make the client's job or life easier. It is essential to remember that the only way to start a good client relationship is to know all you can about the client and his or her needs. Very few business relationships can survive a flawed beginning. So listen and pay attention.

When it's your turn, be careful to avoid using overly technical terms. Don't show off. Otherwise you will see the client's eyes glaze over and you will have lost the job. If you see that happening, come back to something more general and make small talk to make everything comfortable again. Then either let the client resume telling you what you need to hear or continue to explain your services.

To close a sale in the interview process, I use the capsule explanation of the client's needs to outline the things I feel I can do. Then I give the job's approximate cost and ask the client flat out whether to proceed. If the client says, "Yes, it sounds reasonable," we are off and I turn on the billable clock. When clients say, "Well, no, I have to go home and talk to my Aunt Suzie to get her opinion," or something, I say, "Fine, thank you very much." They go off to consult with whomever they feel the need to consult. They may be back or they may not.

"It is a capital mistake to theorize before one has data."

—Sir Arthur Conan Doyle (1859-1930)
Sherlock Holmes in "A Scandal in Bohemia" (1891)

There is another reason to know all about the client. The initial interview is a "free look" for you as well as the client. You want to know all you can about each other. This is a way to avoid some of the later pitfalls of interacting with clients like personality conflicts, emotional entanglements, and ethical disagreements. The first free half-hour's or hour's consultation is an opportunity to size up the client and decide whether or not to enter into a business relationship. If in doubt, get out. That's a hard choice for a beginner. You will soon learn, however, that the grief a doubtful client may cause can overshadow whatever income his or her new business may generate. So, if you sense trouble ahead, do both of you a favor and recommend another practitioner.

Keep Up the Good Work

Once the client retains your services, maintain your good relations: Keep listening! I have learned the hard way that if you have a personal relationship with clients outside the business, as friends or members of your service club or sorority or whatever, you should not take them for granted. Just knowing someone socially does not mean you can ignore him or her in business. Neither does having had a client for a long time. Clients get lost through neglect and complacency. You might think, "Well, I don't have to worry about Old Sam because he's been with me forever and will probably stay with me forever." That's exactly the sort of attitude that can cause Old Sam to go see somebody else. I can say from personal experience that the most painful separations are those brought on when an old client decides your work is not up to the usual standards or you just don't care anymore. That is not great for the self esteem.

Ethical Considerations

Remember, however, that all client relations must fall within the confines of good legal, ethical, and moral behavior. For, as worthy and necessary as clients are, you don't have to take any guff or overstep your own principles just to maintain a large client base. By all means give clients what they feel they want when you can, but do not acquiesce in the commission of a tax fraud or other bad act. If you know or even reasonably suspect that the client is withholding facts or considering a fast one, stay ethical and steer clear of any risk of complicity.

If clients want to commit fraud, it's a personal choice. The best response is to be up front and explain why the proposed course will probably lead to trouble. Bring it out in the open right away. If the client decides to go ahead regardless, then let it be with someone else's advice and assistance.

I might interject that recommending other practitioners holds a danger that I have not directly encountered but bears discussion here. Whenever you refer out an incompatible, too large, or potentially fraudulent client, there is a risk of liability in recommending one specific practitioner. A lawyer I know usually gives his referrals at least three other good lawyers' names to choose from. He had worked with another lawyer who was sued for malpractice for referring a client to what turned out to be an incompetent colleague. It's just something to keep in mind.

Miscellaneous Good Practice

Other requirements for maintaining good client relations are obvious but worth repeating. One is to keep your promises. If you say you will do something by a certain time, do it. Return your telephone calls when you say you will. Be honest about the limitations on your abilities and services. That is a matter of being realistic, not negative. Be sensitive in this regard, too, as to what your services are worth and be aware of market conditions so that you don't overprice them. You will find that out quickly enough.

I find that keeping a vital information sheet inside the front cover of each client's file jacket is very helpful. It contains all a client's identifying information: name, telephone number, address, Social Security Number, date of birth, notes of conversations, and so on. It is also a good place to store time sheets. The more detailed these time sheets are, the better—not only to jog your memory but to show the client how much time and effort goes into your billing.

"The Advice Column"

Getting and keeping clients also means persuading them to follow your advice. The great irony of professional advice-giving is, first, that it is hard to persuade people to pay you for your advice. Then, once you convince them to pay, they may totally ignore you, anyway. They are fully capable of blundering on to do exactly what you advise them against. Then, when the disaster you foretold strikes, they may very well deny having any role in it. Some may even adopt a "shoot the messenger" attitude and blame you.

With new start-up-business clients there is a reason to be especially sensitive to this habit of buying then ignoring advice. A start-up business may offer a chance to get in on the ground floor and help the company succeed. If you have faith in the management or owners, you probably should work for them a little harder and try to ease their burdens early on. There is the prospect that, as the company grows, your business relationship will expand along with it. If, on the other hand, the company ignores your advice, you risk losing it to bankruptcy, failure, or simply giving up. So be liberal and persistent with your time and advice. They are all you have to sell and they can produce a viable if not stellar client.

Finally, when clients ignore your advice and come to grief, resist the temptation to say "I told you so." A client who stuck his or her foot in it will probably deny responsibility in the first place and will want even less to hear about it from you. Instead, empathize with the client's predicament and try to help resolve matters. Then you can stress how things will go better under your careful guidance. This, as you can imagine, calls for a great deal of tact and diplomacy.

From the Annals of Internal Revenue

While income taxes contributed nearly $20.3 million of revenues for fiscal Civil-War year 1864, revenues from the tax on distilled spirits were $30.3 million, and on manufacturers and products were $36.2 million. By 1866, the commission's 4,400 employees took in $311 million in income taxes. Congress began to dismantle the elaborate wartime revenue system in 1867, abandoning the system of rate progression and reducing the tax rate. In 1872 the income tax was abandoned.

From 1868 until 1913 nearly 90 percent of all internal revenue collected in the United States came from taxes on fermented and distilled spirits, and tobacco, then on oleomargarine in 1886 and, in 1899, on opium manufactured domestically for smoking. The last two taxes were intended to be regulatory.

In 1894 the Wilson Tariff Act revived the income tax, but in 1895 the U.S. Supreme Court ruled portions of it unconstitutional, then on a rehearing that same year held the whole income tax unconstitutional because it was not apportioned among the states on the basis of population. As the United States was drawn into the Spanish-American War, Congress in 1898 levied taxes on inheritances, mixed flour, and occupations. It also provided for a number of stamp taxes and increased levies on fermented liquors and tobacco products. Federal revenues again dropped in 1902 as the war receded.

A tax business is seasonal; I want to add "by definition" but can't find a dictionary that has found it out yet. You have to pay very close attention to how you manage your money.

9

Money Matters

THERE are only three things you have to know about money: demanding it, getting it, and keeping it. If you mastered those three perfectly, you wouldn't have a financial worry in the world. You would probably also become one of *Forbes* magazine's 400 richest Americans. While this chapter will not guarantee you fame and fortune—no book I know of can do that—it may impart a better grasp of those three axioms of financial advancement.

How Much Do You Charge?

Everyone would like to have his or her taxes prepared or books balanced for nothing. That is not an option. In pricing your service, market conditions will create an average price and you should probably peg your services close to that average. You can find this average by telephoning the competition and asking, "What do you charge for your bookkeeping service?" "What is your fee structure for tax preparation?"

What the Market Will Bear

What you do is conduct a telephone survey. Find out what services the competition offers and what they charge for them. It will give you a range of prices with a target in the middle to shoot for. You might

Civil War taxpayers lined up at a collector's office.

have to call under pretext of being a potential customer. I don't like subterfuges, but as in any other area of work and life, some of your colleagues will be helpful and willing to share information, and others will be very jealous and protective of their turf. My experience is that if you are collegial and pleasant, they will be more than happy to help out. If you are lucky, you will get the information without the need for pretense and begin to build that needed network in the business.

Your fees will be based on supply and demand as reflected in local prevailing rates. Even if you pick your fee from a range of prevailing rates, what goes into it are the community's prosperity, your acceptance in the community, and the value of your services to the client. "Value to the client" is roughly what the client would pay to have the work done in-house. Much of that is fairly intuitive, but it is worth keeping in mind as you conduct your rates survey. Pay attention to who is giving you the figures. Does the firm seem to be making money, or are its prices too low to do more than cover expenses?

I recommend aiming for that middle pricing target, and not the lower end. This is not a price-cutting business. In retail you may go for the lowest price because a box of soap is a box of soap. In this business, however, you cannot provide the necessary service for your client and stay in business with enough left over to live on if you don't price yourself competitively. You will find, I think, that if you are within the middle range for your geographic location, price will not be an issue except for people who are price shopping. Those are clients, individual or business, that you don't want, anyway. If you are preparing taxes in California, every tax return you sign is a contract liability for at least four years. If you priced yourself on the liability you might incur, you would price your tax returns at $1,200 a return. And you would have only three clients at most. So put yourself in the middle of the pack. What you are providing is professional services; you know what you are talking about; the criteria for selecting you will be your competence as a professional, and not necessarily the price.

The reproducible telephone survey sheets in the Appendix will help gather pricing information. You can use the results of your survey and the profit-and-loss spreadsheet to forecast how many hours' income you will need to reach break-even.

Flat Fees

Clients will expect you to quote them a fixed fee for many routine jobs and for some that may not seem routine when you start out. As with hourly rates, the easiest way to handle flat or fixed fees is to see what the competition charges. Even so, you may find it useful to quote flat fees for a number of jobs. Within six months to a year, you will get pretty good at estimating them. Meanwhile, here's an approach you might take.

One bookkeeper works up a basic schedule of minimum rates for each kind of tax report using a market survey like the one I recommended. Factors affecting the basic rate are the skill and experience of staff members who worked on the job, time needed to prepare the report, whether it is a rush job, whether special services like consulting were involved, *and* the client's customary fee. Thus, a "flat" fee may increase or shrink if the assignment takes more or less time than average or has other unusual features. These calculations will also take account of the client's ability to pay and the value of your services to the client. As stated elsewhere in these pages, you may have to exclude very small businesses that cannot afford a fee that provides a profit and covers its share of expenses.

When setting flat fees for the first time try to quote a tentative price. You can base it on your telephone survey to the extent that you got specific information. When you do a job for a flat fee keep a record of all time actually spent on the account. At month's end multiply the time spent by the appropriate hourly rate. This means you will classify the work done according to the kind of specialization used to do it. One classification may be your own time, another may be your assistant's work-up time, another may be the time to produce the final report. Record each kind of time to the nearest tenth or quarter hour—your choice. Keep those figures as records to help determine what classes of work are involved in each kind of report and how much time each class takes. They will also confirm whether or not the fee is adequate.

Setting flat fees calls for trial and error. If you find yourself in error more often than not, and the fee turns out to be insufficient, discuss it with your client. Try to reach an agreement, and adjust it if the client agrees. If the client does not agree, charge the original rate and say no more. The client has been prepared for an increased fee next time. Keep in mind the tentative nature of flat-fee setting and consider whether first-time inefficiencies may account for any excess costs. Also remember the value of your services to the client. Pricing is necessarily a juggling act to get the best price for you and your client. The fee must provide you income plus operating expenses and profits, and be a good value for the client.

Here is an example of work for one theoretical client: Assume you have set up the books for a small, growing business. You and the proprietor agree to a two- or three-month trial period that will cost the client not more than $200 a month. You figure the rate on the projected average time to do the work each month multiplied by your hourly rates. Remember that the hourly rate should cover each hour's share of operating expenses, your salary or your assistant's, and a profit for the business. It usually takes three months to get a new system operating so that

Next Two Pages:

A two-page 1040W optional short form for wages and salaries appeared for tax years 1959 and 1960 but was abandoned in 1961. In 1965 the forms' design and typography (shown here) were improved on recommendation of a consulting firm hired to suggest a more readable and attractive format.

Form 1040 U.S. Individual Income Tax Return 1965

for the year January 1–December 31, 1965 or other taxable year beginning_____,
1965, ending_____, 19____ US Treasury Department—Internal Revenue Service

▲ Attach Copy B of Form W-2 here

First name and initial (if joint return, use first names and middle initials of both)	Last name	Your social security number (Husband's if joint return)
Home address (Number and street or rural route)		Your occupation & present employer
City, town or post office, and State	Postal ZIP code	Wife's number, if joint return
Enter the name and address used on your return for 1964 (if the same as above, write "Same"). If none filed, give reason. If changing from separate to joint or joint to separate returns, enter 1964 names and addresses.		Wife's occupation & present employer

Filing Status—check one:

- **1a** ☐ Single
- **1b** ☐ Married filing joint return (even if only one had income)
- **1c** ☐ Married filing separately. If your husband or wife is also filing a return give his or her first name and social security number.
- **1d** ☐ Unmarried Head of Household
- **1e** ☐ Surviving widow(er) with dependent child

Exemptions

	Regular	65 or over	Blind	
2a Yourself	☐	☐	☐	Enter number of exemptions checked ▶ ▶ ▶
2b Wife	☐	☐	☐	

3a First names of your dependent children who lived with you._____

_____ Enter number ▶ ↘ ▶

3b Number of other dependents (from page 2 Part I, line 3)

4 Total exemptions claimed . . . . ▶▶▶

Income

If joint return, include all income of both husband and wife

- **5** Wages, salaries, tips, etc. If not shown on attached Forms W-2 attach explanation . ▶
- **6** Other income (from page 2, Part II, line 9) . . . . ▶
- **7** Total (add lines 5 and 6) . . . . ▶
- **8** Adjustments (from page 2, Part III, line 5) . . . . ▶
- **9** Total Income (subtract line 8 from line 7) . . . . ▶

Tax Computation

Figure tax by using either 10 or 11

- **10** Tax Table—if you do not itemize deductions and line 9 is less than $5,000, find your tax from tables in instructions. Do not use lines 11 a, b, c, or d. Enter tax on line 12.
- **11** Tax Rate Schedule—
- **11a** If you itemize deductions, enter total from page 2, Part IV . . . . ▶
  If you do not itemize deductions, and line 9 is $5,000 or more enter the larger of:
  (1) 10 percent of line 9 or;
  (2) $200 ($100 if married and filing separate return) plus $100 for each exemption claimed on line 4, above.
  The deduction computed under (1) or (2) is limited to $1,000 ($500 if married and filing separate return).
- **11b** Subtract line 11a from line 9 . . . .
- **11c** Multiply total number of exemptions on line 4, above, by $600 . . . . . .
- **11d** Subtract line 11c from line 11b. Enter balance on this line. (Figure your tax on this amount by using tax rate schedule on page 11 of instructions.) Enter tax on line 12. .

Tax Credits Payments

- **12** Tax (from either Tax Table, see line 10, or Tax Rate Schedule, see line 11) . . . ▶
- **13** Total credits (from page 2, Part V, line 5) . . . . ▶
- **14** Income tax (subtract line 13 from line 12) . . . . ▶
- **15** Self-employment tax (Schedule C-3 or F-1) . . . . ▶
- **16** Total tax (add lines 14 and 15) . . . . ▶
- **17a** Total Federal income tax withheld (attach Forms W-2) . . . ▶
- **17b** 1965 Estimated tax payments . . . . ▶
  (Include 1964 overpayment allowed as a credit) (Office where paid)
- **17c** Total (add lines 17a and 17b) . . . .

If either you or your wife worked for more than one employer see page 5 of instructions

Tax Due or Refund

- **18** If payments (line 17c) are less than tax (line 16), enter Balance Due. Pay in full with this return ▶
- **19** If payments (line 17c) are larger than tax (line 16) enter Overpayment . . . . ▶▶▶
- **20** Amount of line 19 you wish credited to 1966 Estimated Tax . . . .
- **21** Subtract line 20 from 19. Apply to: ☐ U.S. Savings Bonds, with excess refunded or ☐ Refund only

▲ Attach Check or Money Order here ▶

Under penalties of perjury, I declare that I have examined this return, including accompanying schedules and statements, and to the best of my knowledge and belief it is true, correct, and complete. If prepared by a person other than taxpayer, his declaration is based on all information of which he has any knowledge.

▲ Sign here ▶ If joint return, BOTH HUSBAND AND WIFE MUST SIGN even if only one had income. Date____

Sign here Signature of preparer other than taxpayer.   Address   Date____

PART I. Exemptions Complete only for dependents claimed on line 3b, page 1   Form 1040 1965 Page 2

(a) NAME(If more space is needed attach schedule)	(b) Relationship	(c) Months lived in your home. If born or died during year write "B" or "D"	(d) Did dependent have income of $600 or more?	(e) Amount YOU furnished for dependent's support. If 100% write "ALL"	(f) Amount furnished by OTHERS including dependent.
1				$	$
2					

3 Total number of dependents listed above. Enter here and on page 1, line 3b ▶▶▶▶ ☐

PART II. Income from all sources other than wages, salaries, etc.

Dividends and Other Distributions

A Gross amount

B Nontaxable and capital gain distributions

C Subtract item B from item A. Give details in lines 1a through 1d

Explanation of C (Write (H). (W). (J). for stock held by husband, wife, or jointly)

1a Qualifying dividends (name of payer)

Total qualifying

1b Subtract $100. If joint return see instructions

1c Balance (but not less than zero)

1d Nonqualifying dividends (name of payer)

Total nonqualifying

2 Total dividends (add lines 1c and 1d) ▶▶▶

3 Interest (name of payer)

Total interest income ▶▶▶▶

4 Pensions and annuities, rents and royalties, partnerships, & estates or trusts (Schedule B)

5 Business income (Schedule C) ▶

6 Sale or exchange of property (Schedule D)

7 Farm income (Schedule F) ▶

8 Other sources (state nature)

Total other sources ▶▶▶▶

9 Add lines 2 through 8. Enter here and on page 1 line 6, ▶▶▶▶

PART III. Adjustments

1 "Sick pay" if included in line 5, page 1 (attach Form 2440 or other required statement)

2 Moving expenses (attach Form 3903)

3 Employee business expense (attach Form 2106 or other statement)

4 Payments by self-employed persons to retirement plans, etc. (attach Form 2950SE)

5 Total adjustments (lines 1 through 4). Enter here and on page 1, line 8

EXPENSE ACCOUNT INFORMATION—If you had an expense allowance or charged expenses to your employer, check here ☐ and see page 7 of instructions.

PART IV. Itemized deductions—Use only if you do not use tax table or standard deduction.

Medical and dental expense.—Attach itemized list. Do not enter any expense compensated by insurance or otherwise. NOTE: if you or your wife are 65 or over, or if either has a dependent parent 65 or over, see page 8 of instructions for possible larger deduction:

1 Enter excess, if any, of medicine and drugs over 1% of line 9, page 1 (See note above)

2 Other medical, dental expenses (include hospital insurance premiums)

3 Total (add lines 1 and 2)

4 Enter 3% of line 9, page 1 (See note above)

5 Subtract line 4 from line 3; see page 8 of instructions for maximum limitation ▶

Contributions.—Cash—including checks, money orders, etc. (Itemize)

1 Total cash contributions

2 Other than cash (see instructions for required statement). Enter total of such items here

3 Total contributions (add lines 1 and 2—see instructions for limitations) ▶▶▶▶

Taxes.—Real estate $

State and local gasoline $

General sales $

State and local income $

Personal property $

Total taxes ▶▶▶▶

Interest expense.—Home mortgage $

Other (itemize)

Total interest expense ▶▶▶▶

Other deductions.—(see page 9 of instructions)

Total other deductions ▶▶▶▶

TOTAL DEDUCTIONS (for page 1, line 11a) ▶

PART V. Credits

1 Retirement income credit (Schedule B)

2 Investment credit (Form 3468)

3 Foreign tax credit (Form 1116)

4 Tax-free covenant bonds credit

5 Total credits (add lines 1 through 4). Enter here and on page 1, line 13

the client has his documents ready when you need them. Assume again that at the end of three months it takes 10 to 11 hours to do the job. You tell the client you can do the work for, say, $250, not $200, a month, and the client agrees. Eight or 10 months down the road you do the work in about nine and a half hours because you and the client have gotten more efficient in handling it. One way to look at savings is as additional profit that the firm is entitled to. If in some months it takes longer to do the work, whether it's your fault or not, you can absorb the added cost.

In any case, it is a good idea to reserve the right at the end of the trial period to review the price quotation and adjust it if necessary. Some practitioners do not quote fixed fees for monthly work because many clients start off uncertain about the value of the services. As they gain confidence in the process, most begin to appreciate its value and give the firm more work than originally bargained for. Some expect you to do the extra work for the original amount, which can make flat fees a hard bargain to shake.

Another bookkeeper recommends studying the client carefully to find out what information about the business the client needs and wants. It might be a drugstore or other business with discrete profit centers that needs a departmental analysis. When you have studied how to set up the books calculate all the time spent making monthly trial balances, bank reconciliations, profit and loss statements and tax returns. Even if you don't work for a flat fee, you need to analyze the job to do it well, and you need to know how long it will take and roughly what it will cost the client.

When you are familiar with a client's books, tax preparation is fairly easy. Since you keep the books throughout the year, you can adjust and correct as you go to simplify the year-end statement. It is a real help in the tax season. My office can handle many times the volume of returns for regular clients than once-a-year clients. Regular clients get a break for tax preparation, because, knowing their books, it is easier to prepare their taxes. Clients that come in once a year for taxes are charged more.

A Living Wage

A final word about pricing, then we'll move on. If you start out charging low, you won't be able to raise your rates without losing clients, possibly all of them. The alternative is to keep working but for nothing. There is an entity right around the corner from me. Its principals work all the time. I mean, they have mountains of stuff to plow through and process. But they aren't making any money. They have a lot of activity, but precious little reward. So charge a sensible rate right off the bat. When you do get all the clients you need they will provide you with a decent income.

Collecting the Money

It is no good working for nothing. It doesn't do you any good to have worthless clients, and there are plenty of them. You are better off, and sometimes the client is better off, if you turn down the job. It is not easy at first to judge up front, but after awhile you develop a sixth sense of who will and won't pay. When the little hairs on the back of my neck stand up while talking to a prospective client, I often refer such clients out. I tell them that "I can do this for you but I can't do it as economically as Joe or whoever around the corner." I accomplish two things. I tell them that I am too expensive and I give them somewhere else to go. Joe doesn't always appreciate it, but it's a one way to get out of an impossible obligation. If I were Joe, I would have a special pre-paid fee arrangement for this kind of client.

Prepaid Fees and Retainers

As a matter of fact, requiring deposits and retainers is a good way to do business with almost all your clients. Traditional practice is to bill after the fact. You do the work, submit the bill, and then wait to get paid. The retainer idea is one of actually billing ahead. When you have an idea how much a job will bill out at, you collect money for it up front, operate on it and when you have put in the hours that consume the deposit, then you bill the client for as much more as you need to complete the job. It is a much better way to operate, because clients are pre-paid and you are not running the risk of hanging in the wind for work you have done.

This isn't as outlandish as it may sound. It may be different from what people have come to think is common practice, but I think it has merit. Even the newspaper carrier bills in advance these days. It is also a way to smooth out your cash flow. It doesn't leave you in a position of having done the job, with payment coming late or never. It keeps you from having to be a bill collector, too. Some facility for estimating fees, as with flat-fee billing, helps here. If handled right and the client accepts it, it reduces money tensions between you and your client and doesn't interfere with client relations. Further, I think it establishes the expectation that you are a professional, that your client is a professional, and that you are going to deliver on your end of the bargain.

Prepayment probably works best for a flat fee kind of job, like preparing a tax return. It can also be modified for an ongoing service like bookkeeping for a business if there is, say, a quarterly retainer fee that precedes doing the job. With open-ended kinds of work, you have to use your judgment and calculate how much to ask for as the work progresses. Some state bar associations require lawyers to set up a trust account at their bank for depositing client retainers. The idea is that those funds are never commingled with the lawyers' general account until they are withdrawn as fees or to cover costs. Each client has a trust account balance, on which the lawyer keeps a ledger sheet, and the bar requires that the ledger sheets and trust accounts balance at the end of every month. Obviously, this entails a little work, but not much more than collecting bills, and it is much less frustrating than chasing no-pays and slow-pays.

Checks and Collection

By the time you have screened your clients and taken them on you can probably accept their checks without too much fuss. It could be downright insulting to go through a credit check. If you take an up-front deposit, this won't be much of an issue. There will be cases, however, where clients don't pay and the debt gets old. Either you will know a client well enough to telephone and talk the client into paying, or it is a valuable client who is honest and trustworthy but for some reason cannot pay. My inclination is to give the client the benefit of the doubt.

I try to work with the client and let him or her know that I understand the situation. There are times when the money simply is not collectible, and you have to write it off. Some good clients of mine, a husband and wife, are a perfect example of this. He was in construction, and when the construction business declined he had to declare bankruptcy. These were not bad people. They had just come up against it through no fault of their own. You have to have some understanding and compassion for these cases.

If you take precautions and work with a client, bad debts should be very uncommon. It does happen, however, and it happens in every business. The point is to try to make sure the bad debts are little ones and you don't have to write off the big ones. Over the years I have eaten several thousand dollars of bad debt, but so be it. I have never subscribed to using collection agencies or other means of hounding people. It's a matter of personal choice. I don't find going through a collection process worth the aggravation and discomfort. If a client is giving me a runaround and not paying, I just write it off. I send back the client's material and tell them to go somewhere else.

Our Constitution is in actual operation; everything appears to promise that it will last; but in this world nothing can be said to be certain, except death and taxes.

—Benjamin Franklin (1706-1790)
Letter, November 13, 1789

Handling Receivables

That doesn't mean you shouldn't be businesslike about your receivables. Always send out notices. Successful fee arrangements depend on follow-up. Keep even your prepaid clients advised of their bills every month. If you are managing your accounts properly, you shouldn't be hanging in the wind for more than a few hundred dollars on any given account. If you are out for a couple of thousand bucks on an account, you had better be darned certain of that account. If it goes sour, it is your own fault for being careless. The sensible approach today is to computerize your accounts receivable and send out notices. Use a system to date receivables. Set a cut-off date when you will no longer perform until paid. I always send notices after 30 days and 60 days. Then, if I don't get a response, I telephone. If telephoning doesn't produce results, then I kiss it off.

It helps to put some sort of late-payment penalty or interest charge on the bill for payment after 30 days. You inform the client that if payment is not made in 30 days you will levy a late fee at a certain rate, usually with a minimum of $10 or $25. It should be enough to get the bill paid but not such that it runs afoul of your state's usury laws. Usury laws vary among states; in some the law may not even pertain to the interest on your bill. Another approach might be to offer a discount for prompt payment, but that can eat into revenues if it is too generous.

Managing Your Money

A tax business is seasonal; I want to add "by definition" but can't find a dictionary that has found it out yet. There are periods of intense activity from February through April, and there are slack periods, most notably in late summer. I find that along about August things get pretty quiet. That is great for catching up on every incremental little goal, but it is hard on income. It makes you pay very close attention to how you manage your money.

Spend Wisely, Not Too Well

Stick to a budget. Look for cost-cutting opportunities like buying supplies at a discount from mail order suppliers or warehouse retailers, but be careful not to buy more than you can use. The classic example is business cards. Printers tell you the usual minimum amount is 1,000 cards. Buy 250. Before you use up those business cards the business probably will have expanded, and you will have a new address, a new telephone number, new services or associates, and I don't know how many boxes of worthless business cards. There is nothing you can do with them. They won't burn; they sit there like bricks. The same is true of a lot of supplies. You can buy cheap in bulk but it takes months, years, to use up bulk. Don't put your money in paper bricks.

Don't splurge on office furniture and equipment. Buy used. I said this before, but it's worth repeating. If you forgot about it, go back to page 30 and read it again.

Take discounts for early payment on your bills wherever possible. Keep overhead costs like rent, utilities, and telephone service under control. Pay expenses that nourish the business like directory advertising and target advertising.

Get dependable insurance coverage without over-insuring. Even if you use a broker rather than a salesman, ask about prices as well as the company's reputation for paying claims. Remember the broker is there to steer you to an *effective* insurance purchase. If nobody can recommend or knows a carrier you select on price alone, check to see if your state's insurance commissioner has received any complaints against it.

Prepare things for lawyers and other professionals. For example, you will find that the least desirable clients are those who bring you their records in a shoe box. They take the most time and are often are the least likely to pay you. I always tell these clients they need some preliminary bookkeeping. I give them an outline of categories for organizing the information and I give them two choices. I will be happy to organize all the material for them, I will be equally happy to charge them a $25-per-hour bookkeeping service fee to do it, and I estimate that it will take three to five hours. Or they can take their shoe boxes home to do it themselves, and we can make another appointment for next week. It's usually a strong incentive for the client to save professional fees. If they say, go ahead, do it anyway, I will have at least prepared them for an extra $75 to $125 fee. If they go away, I don't feel I have lost anything.

By the same token, other professionals won't like dealing with *you* if you dump a shoe box of your problems on their desks. The more prepared you are, and the better you have thought through your needs, the less time that professional has to spend on your job and the less he or she will charge you for it.

Employees as a Management Tool

I have stressed the importance of a good support staff, but don't hire office help until you need it. Once you hit the point of needing help, however, don't hesitate to hold your nose and jump right in. There are only so many hours in a day and only so much energy you can expend. It is much more effective to spend that time generating $75 per hour, or whatever your fee is, and pay someone else $10 per hour to do all the other stuff. After you have been going awhile you will reach a threshold where you will decide that you want to take on an assistant and let that person handle some of the necessary but less appealing tasks. That will free up your time to do more client development, interviewing, or actual case work, depending on where your strengths lie. Computers have minimized much of the tedium for sole practitioners, but at some point, if you are successful, you will need to take on another person. There are two reasons why you should not hesitate.

First, as mentioned, it will free your time to generate more revenue. Second, it creates a tangible incentive for that extra revenue by increasing your responsibility to develop the business and provide not only for yourself but for your employee.

Once you have a staff, managing your money includes keeping them busy all year around so that they pay their way. It requires setting up day-to-day bookkeeping tasks like write-up business. If you do monthly or quarterly accounts you can keep one person at posting and maintaining client files on a regular basis. In the busy season you can hire seasonal help. Commonly a going practice will take on some tax preparers for the season with the understanding that it is for a fixed term and a contract job, not a year-around position. This is the other side of getting started by signing on with an established firm for seasonal work. It works to both parties' advantage.

Keeping the Money

Maintain the cash flow and stay liquid. There may be some temptation at the end of the season—for instance, when you have collected a large portion of the annual revenues and have a big wad of cash in your checking account—to invest those funds or go on a vacation. In the initial stages, however, leave the money in the checking account until you have six months' worth of operating expenses. If you have revenues above that, you might consider committing them for a longer period of time to take advantage of higher interest rates. But first get a good six months' cushion in the account. For some of us it may help to categorize income into, say, 20 percent as a benefits cushion, 10 percent to reinvest in the business, 10 percent for an untouchable safety net, and—live a little!—five percent for fun.

From the Annals of Internal Revenue

Pressure for a new income tax began to mount at the beginning of the 20th Century, although wealthier Americans tended to view its progressive character as socialistic. Popular sentiment, however, was growing against the wealthy. President William Howard Taft worked out a compromise with Congress by 1909, recommending that Congress propose an amendment letting the federal government tax incomes without apportioning the tax among the states.

In August 1909 the two-percent excise tax that Taft proposed on corporate incomes above $5,000 became law, with the added benefit of forestalling the need for an income tax until it could be constitutionally established. The 16th Amendment became part of the Constitution when in February 1913 Wyoming's ratification as the 36th state provided the needed consent of three-fourths of all the states.

A tariff bill with income tax sections became law in October 1913. It levied a one-percent tax on net personal incomes over $3,000, with a surtax to six percent on incomes over $500,000. It also repealed the corporation tax of 1909 and created a new corporate income tax. It was just in time for World War I.

While America did not go to war until 1917, the government needed new income to make up for declining imports from the warring parties. The war Revenue Acts of 1917 and 1918 were sweeping measures that raised huge sums to finance the war effort. From 1903 to 1915, the average yearly income tax collection was $281 million. It increased almost tenfold in the 12 years following 1915 to $2.7 billion. The 1918 law also codified all existing tax laws and created a progressive income tax up to 77 percent. It was also the first to lower double taxation of individuals and corporations with foreign income, and to liberalize the deduction for depletion of natural resources. It also taxed child labor in an attempt to destroy it. The U.S. Supreme Court held this last provision unconstitutional in 1922.

If you don't believe your work is beneficial to you, to your clients, and the community at large—then all the calendars and New Year's resolutions in the world won't help you work better.

10

Good Work Habits

GOOD work habits are essential in the practical day-to-day development and operation of any small business, including a bookkeeping and tax practice. This is especially true during the tax season. But, instead of arising from a mechanical arrangement of time and tasks on a calendar, good work habits require a psychological and emotional commitment to set up your time and tasks *so that they work for you*. That is advice you don't find in every "how to succeed" book.

Self-Discipline and All That

Before discussing how to become efficient, here are my gratuitous thoughts for putting efficiency in its place. First of all, I am not the best time budgeter in the world. I apologize, but I don't think it is a big deal in the greater scheme of things. It's important, but I don't let it run my life. Conventional wisdom says that budgeting time involves establishing and following a productive work schedule. It is what my father used to refer to as "self-discipline." It can also be a trap if viewed out of the context of a happy, useful life. You have to ask yourself, What is the self-discipline for? I think that if you are truly interested in the tasks at hand and perceive that what you are doing is beneficial, not only to you but to your clients and the larger community, you will be drawn to doing the work rather than having to drive yourself. It reminds me of the saying that it is easier to pull a string than to push it. All those books and seminars and tapes about making a schedule, sticking to it, building efficiency, and so on, smack of trying to push the string.

You have to pull a string, and you should be pulled by your belief and confidence that what you are doing is important. If you don't believe it, then all the efficiency measures and New Year's resolutions in the world won't make you any better at work that isn't compelling and fun. No matter how perfect your calendars and schedules look on paper you will waste your time—and your life. When you and your work come first, the schedules and calendars follow.

Okay, assuming we are all working at what we love, the next step is to fit the routine to us, not the other way around. The first step is to learn your "bio-rhythms," for lack of a better word. You have to know yourself. Knowing yourself, try to assign the most demanding tasks to the time when you run at peak efficiency. If you are a morning person, set important appointments or interviews and tough problems for the morning, or the afternoon if you are an evening person. Put off the easy, less demanding work—those pieces of cake—for your low-ebb hours.

Scheduling for You

If you are starting out as a sole practitioner and doing everything from answering the phone to mopping floors, you need to provide some time—preferably your off-hours—and exert discipline to take care of the menial, boring, but necessary tasks. Eventually, you may be able to delegate some of them to a good and worthy assistant. I have been fortunate in that respect and I recommend it.

Once your routine tasks are scheduled to best advantage, then you can organize your peak time. To organize appointments I have always found it helpful to keep an appointment book. In my case it is a day-date calendar that I keep on my desk. Whenever I make appointments I put down not only the client's name but the phone number, too, in case I need to postpone a meeting. Then I can call up to rearrange things without having to dig through the files. If you have an assistant, both of you should have a calendar and they should match. It's a way to double-check your appointments.

The appointment calendar is your first step to good organization. The second step is budgeting your time. Notice that I put this pretty far down on the list. I am afraid I fall far short of perfection where budgeting time is concerned. That's all right. Everyone has a time-budgeting problem, more or less. The way to overcome it without becoming an obsessive clock watcher is to notice how and where time gets lost. Make notes, if necessary. If you didn't keep notes, at least think back over where things got delayed. Then, rather than forcing yourself into the wrong-shaped hole, use technology or support personnel to make up for your weaknesses. It can be done. Use all the tools available to organize the business so that time is your servant, not a master.

To business that we love we rise betime,
And go to't with delight.

—William Shakespeare (1564-1616)
ANTONY AND CLEOPATRA (Act IV, Sc. 4, Line 20.)

I think, for example, a little palm-sized tape recorder is an excellent tool for dictating letters and making notes when I can turn those tapes over to a competent assistant to organize them and make them useful. Otherwise, it is just talking into the air. Before you have any staff, you will have to keep you own notes and write your own letters. Computer calendar and word-processing software make it easier, and as a beginner your work will not take up all of your time and an assistant's. But be aware that note-taking and letter-writing does not directly generate income. Recognize it as a cost of doing business from the beginning and calculate when it becomes economical to hire the support staff to do it for you at a lower hourly rate.

I find that usually my problem is underestimating how long a task will take, or beginning something that takes twice as long as I estimated. As I became more familiar with the work, I made adjustments and allowances to build a tighter time budget. In the beginning, I had to learn what my strengths and weaknesses were, just as I learned what my most productive time of day was. From that point on it was a matter of concentrating on my strengths and focusing them on the tasks at hand.

The most vital tool in this business is the telephone. It is your link with the outside world. It is often your main source of communication with clients and colleagues. You need to know how to use the telephone and present yourself well over it. You must impress your staff with the importance of using it well, also. You should also screen potential employees for the impression they will make on it.

Once on the telephone or face-to-face with a client, limit your conversation. It is all right, even advisable, to develop a cordial relationship with clients, but don't waste time chattering. I don't have that particular problem but I know people who do. I think it is worth mentioning as a potential time waster.

Facing the Seasonal Rush

Rush work and busy seasons are a permanent feature of this business, and your ability to handle peak loads efficiently needs careful planning and organization. Each of us handles the workload differently. I offer the following suggestions as possibilities for managing through the busy season. You may not want to use them all. I don't.

First, standardize your stationery and supplies so there are no more than four or five sizes of working paper. The fewer sizes, the better. Also, use paper of a uniform standard grade and quality to ensure a reasonably continuous future supply. Keep a book of all your forms for your own and your clients' use. Have a master chart of accounts that can be altered and adapted to each new client's needs. If you like detail, have each employee keep a time card to record all productive time spent on each client's file. That time will be posted to a time record for each client that you bill by the hour. The total time for each employee multiplied by the employee's rate is the basis for your charge to the client. One popular time-and-billing computer program for this is *Timeslips*. Train your assistants to handle all details and routine work. Standardize how you file working papers so they are in the same sequence for all your clients.

One thing I do in tax season is discourage drop-in trade. This is very important. I schedule all my appointments and spread them out. I don't want people waiting in the reception room, getting frustrated and wasting their time and mine. Even then I will adjust the appointments, when necessary, to accommodate the clients.

Finally, just so you don't waste all this efficiency, proofread your reports. Better, have someone else proofread them. Clients will often fixate on minor errors; so don't let typos detract from the high quality of your work.

Setting Interim and Long Range Goals

How do you eat an elephant? One bite at a time. In any business, and especially in this business around tax time, it is not uncommon to feel overwhelmed by the tasks at hand and the volume of work that needs to get done. That is when you need to remember the adage of how to eat an elephant. When you find yourself faced with an overwhelming task, scale back to your immediate short-term goals to achieve a smaller task. Perhaps scale back even that first task, whatever it is—whether reviewing a client's file or writing a letter—by setting small incremental goals and doing each one. Sometimes having a tightly budgeted schedule can be counter-productive. It can make the volume of work facing you seem monolithic and insuperable. If you develop a habit of nibbling away at any given task you can achieve larger, even grandiose goals pretty much without noticing. The work will get done, as it always does. What matters is whether you feel good about it at the time.

Another Elephant

I am obviously a believer in setting incremental goals that will lead toward larger achievements. Instead of establishing a reference point somewhere out in the future and then worrying about how to build the bridge from "Here" to "There," I decide to lay down a plank at a time.

If you don't get exactly to "There" with this approach, it's because you learn as you go and make suitable adjustments. Rather than saying "I am starting with zero revenue now and in six months I want to be bringing in $10,000 a month," say "Today I can contact this person or the other with the likelihood that it will generate $200 worth of business." That is more realistic and productive.

From the Annals of Internal Revenue

Following the Armistice in 1918, the familiar pattern of retrenchment began. Government in the 1920s stressed economy, cost containment, and a balanced budget. For some, prosperity reigned, the stock market boomed, and the decade roared. Although Congress cut tax rates five times, receipts remained high.

The Volstead Act for National Prohibition in 1919 followed ratification of the 18th Amendment. Internal Revenue was selected to eradicate alcohol, and did so until the Justice Department took over in 1930. The reason for its selection, other than its experience since 1862 in enforcing alcohol laws, is unclear. It went to work on bootleggers, moonshiners, speakeasies, and racketeers. In 1925 some 3,700 Internal Revenue employees made 77,000 arrests under the prohibition provisions and seized property valued at more than $11 million. In 1931, using a bureau undercover agent, it collected evidence sufficient to convict Al Capone of tax evasion. He was sentenced to 11 years in prison and died there.

In 1927 a special advisory committee in the Commissioner's office began working to reduce the volume of cases pending before the U.S. Board of Tax Appeals, predecessor to the U.S. Tax Court. Now known as the Appeals Division, the committee provided a quick and economical resolution to tax disputes.

*You may identify the perfect employee already working for somebody else. Once you decide to hire, go ahead: **Steal 'em!***

11

Employees

AT some point, if the business is successful, you will have to decide whether or not to take on staff, either to expand the business or just keep up with demands on it as it evolves. Once you have more clients than you can handle alone, you can probably clear a profit on an assistant's salary. That happens in two, perhaps three, ways. One is that an assistant frees you from doing routine, less remunerative work and lets you concentrate on charging professional fees for more of your time. The other is it gives you time to generate more business and bring in even more clients. An added benefit is your ability to take more time off to do valuable community work, which may also generate more business, if indirectly, while your assistant handles many of the office's operating needs.

Computer technology allows the sole practitioner to do much more work than was possible in the past. Depending on your own wants and needs you may find those technologies and tools enough to eliminate the need for employees. But usually that will work only up to a certain point. From there on you will need to examine your strengths and preferences very closely. You may decide to hire someone who can supplement your efforts and do the things you don't want to do or cannot do. You will at least need someone to take care of the routine matters.

When to Hire

The first rule of hiring is not to hire until you have to. I am sure none of you have this problem, but some people are inclined to hire support staff because they believe they are so darned important they need a staff to make them look good. Be careful that mimicking someone else's ego doesn't lure you into that trap. The way to determine if you need help is whether or not the business's administrative tasks are taking up time you could otherwise bill out at the higher rate for bookkeeping or tax preparation. In my case, I bill at $75 per hour and it doesn't make sense for me to type letters or send out bills and the like when someone else can do it for me at $10 or $15 per hour while I am bringing in $75.

If you see a sufficient demand for your billable hours—that is, if you have clients and the prospect of getting more—you can do a straightforward economic analysis. A review of your activities and expenditure of time over the past few months should be sufficient.

Oliver Wendell Holmes, one of our nation's greatest judges, once wrote "Taxes are what we pay for civilized society." . . . He did not say whether his enthusiasm included filling out tax forms.

—Mortimer M. Caplin, Commissioner of Internal Revenue, Letter to Taxpayers in 1963 tax instructions

---

There is often a psychological threshold to cross, too. At some point you may notice when you are handling everything that things are slowing down. The telephone will ring or the front door will open right in the middle of a project. You can't get anything done. When the practice gets busy and your management of it begins to appear inefficient, that is the time to cross the psychological threshold and get help.

Once you decide to hire, proceed with caution. People are easy to hire but hard to fire. This is true if you are someone with some humanity and compassion. Like me you would probably find it hard to say, "I'm sorry but your services are no longer needed." There are also technical and legal considerations. And you will have to be aware of the rules of employment and the requirement that you fire for cause.

An obvious consideration in hiring is to be sure that the employee will make the company more money. You have to sit down and sharpen a pencil and realize that there are more costs to having an employee than simply the hourly wage. There will be additional taxes. You have to pick up your half of the social security tax, pay disability, pay workers' compensation, and consider some benefits. You may not have to offer benefits at first, but at some point if you have a good employee and want to keep him or her, you will have to address the issues of retirement, health care, vacations, sick leave, and so forth. A rough rule of thumb in my experience is that the actual cost of an employee is usually about twice the hourly wage.

Temporaries

In large urban areas it may be possible to "rent" your employees by using temporary help or temporary services. This is certainly an option for tax season when you may need a receptionist or someone to handle correspondence. If you want help at the end of the year to gear up for the tax season, you can bring someone in for three to six weeks on a temporary basis. If your practice allows this as an option, it has the advantage of including employee costs and benefits in the fee. You will pay more on an hourly basis, including the agency's fee, but you will not be responsible for sick leave, vacation, health care, and the like. On the other hand, you will not be able to develop a trusty and devoted sidekick who will help run the business.

The other "temporary" employees are the contract bookkeepers who work during tax season. Hire them early and train them as much as possible. Make it clear that they make as valuable a contribution to the firm as permanent employees and treat them like that. This probably doesn't need saying, but you should treat even employment agency "temps" as well as your own temporary staff. They are often the people your clients meet when they deal with your company. Every employee should make an impression as good as—or better than—you would for your business.

Although you may find an economic advantage in hiring temporary help, be careful not to project a "temporary" appearance to your clients and the public. The person at the front desk is representing you and your company, and a temporary employee may have his or her own personal or professional agenda. It may not entirely jibe with yours. This is still a workable option for a practitioner who is primarily a tax preparer and who is busy mainly during the tax season. The need for temporary help may also provide an opportunity to employ a spouse during the busy season.

The Job Description

Even with a bookkeeping practice in addition to tax preparation, there may not be enough routine administrative work to keep a full-time employee busy beyond the season. The answer is to find someone with bookkeeping skills who can generate revenue during the non-tax season.

My feeling is that in this business, your employee should be considered part of the business, not just a secretary or receptionist or typist. Rather than defining this employee's activities narrowly, I would aim for a well rounded position just slightly below a partner's. A true assistant is just that: someone who has the skill to do all the routine work and some bookkeeping too, including his or her own employee forms and reporting. Hire this person to do the stuff you don't want to do. It is not a burden on the employee. It's a double benefit; I pay my assistant for the time she spends doing her own paperwork and it does not take up my time.

In addition to a wage, I offer my employee referral bonuses. An employee can and should be a source of potential referrals. The woman I have in my office brings in all kinds of business. I distinguish between economic recognition, like production and referral bonuses, and bonuses that are essentially gifts. I think a referral or production bonus has a place in a business by instilling an entrepreneurial spirit in an employee. I'm an entrepreneur, out there beating the bushes to get clients and doing the work. I think that employees who participate in the enterprise ought to be recognized and compensated for it. Bonuses like this work very well and are well spent.

Finding Good Employees

Now that you know what the ideal employee should be and do, the question is how to find one. Like everything in this business, an employee search is on a personal level. I have worked in other environments

---

Facing Page:

Changes from 1965 included a seven-page questionnaire form, 1040Q, in 1966, the introduction of color to the forms in 1968, a half-page 1040A printed front and back, and in 1977 the return of a one-sided, one-page 1040A shown here.

Form **1040A**	Department of the Treasury—Internal Revenue Service **U.S. Individual Income Tax Return**	**1977**		

Use IRS label. Otherwise, print or type.	First name and initial (if joint return, give first names and initials of both)		Last name	Your social security number
	Present home address (Number and street, including apartment number, or rural route)		For Privacy Act Notice, see page 9 of Instructions.	Spouse's social security no.
	City, town or post office, State and ZIP code		Occupation	Yours ▶
				Spouse's ▶

Presidential Election Campaign Fund ▶	Do you want $1 to go to this fund?.	Yes	No	Note: *Checking "Yes" will not increase your tax or reduce your refund.*
	If joint return, does your spouse want $1 to go to this fund?	Yes	No	

Filing Status
Check Only One Box

1 ☐ Single   2 ☐ Married filing joint return (even if only one had income)
3 ☐ Married filing separately. If spouse is also filing, give spouse's social security number in the space above and enter full name here ▶..
4 ☐ Unmarried Head of Household. Enter qualifying name ▶ · See page 6 of Instructions.

Exemptions
Always check the "Yourself" box. Check other boxes if they apply.

5a ☐ Yourself   ☐ 65 or over   ☐ Blind   Enter number of boxes checked on 5a and b ▶ ☐
b ☐ Spouse   ☐ 65 or over   ☐ Blind
c First names of your dependent children who lived with you ▶.............   Enter number of children listed ▶ ☐

d Other dependents: (1) Name	(2) Relationship	(3) Number of months lived in your home.	(4) Did dependent have income of $750 or more?	(5) Did you provide more than one-half of dependent's support?	Enter number of other dependents ▶ ☐

6 Total number of exemptions claimed . . . .   Add numbers entered in boxes above ▶ ☐

7	Wages, salaries, tips, and other employee compensation. (Attach Forms W–2. If unavailable, see page 11 of Instructions)	7	
8	Interest income (see page 4 of Instructions).	8	
9a	Dividends............ 9b Less exclusion .... Balance ▶ (See pages 4 and 11 of Instructions)	9c	
10	Adjusted gross income (add lines 7, 8, and 9c). If under $8,000, see page 2 of Instructions on "Earned Income Credit." If eligible, enter child's name ▶	10	
11a	Credit for contributions to candidates for public office. Enter one-half of amount paid but do not enter more than $25 ($50 if joint return)	11a	

IF YOU WANT IRS TO FIGURE YOUR TAX, PLEASE STOP HERE AND SIGN BELOW.

b	Total Federal income tax withheld (if line 7 is larger than $16,500, see page 12 of Instructions)	11b	
c	Earned income credit (from page 2 of Instructions)	11c	
12	Total (add lines 11a, b, and c)	12	
13	Tax on the amount on line 10. (See Instructions for line 13 on page 12, then find your tax in Tax Tables on pages 14–25.)	13	
14	If line 12 is larger than line 13, enter amount to be **REFUNDED TO YOU** . . . . ▶	14	
15	If line 13 is larger than line 12, enter **BALANCE DUE.** Attach check or money order for full amount payable to "Internal Revenue Service." Write social security number on check or money order . . ▶	15	

Under penalties of perjury, I declare that I have examined this return, including accompanying schedules and statements, and to the best of my knowledge and belief, it is true, correct, and complete. Declaration of preparer (other than taxpayer) is based on all information of which preparer has any knowledge.

Please Sign

▶ Your signature _____ Date _____

Paid preparer's signature and identifying number (see Instructions)
....

▶ Spouse's signature (if filing jointly, BOTH must sign even if only one had income)

Paid preparer's address (or employer's name, address, and identifying number)

(left margin, vertical text:) Please Attach Copy B of Forms W–2 Here   Please Attach Check or Money Order Here

where I was responsible for interviewing potential employees. It is very tough to interview someone and get a true impression of the person. Until you work with people for six months, you have no idea what they are capable of, or what strengths and weaknesses they have.

To find an employee I always rely on word of mouth, and I recommend it to anyone else who wants to bring someone into the practice who will essentially share it. If you are in the market to hire a good person, spread the word. Talk to friends. Talk to colleagues. Talk to your professionals, your doctor, your lawyer—anybody you deal with. The person whose name pops up most often is the one you want to contact. Talk to clients, too, especially those who own businesses. They are an excellent source for finding good people. Occasionally, one will have a good employee and for some reason have to cut back and let that person go. The client may approach you about not wanting to leave him or her out in the cold. That's who you want: The employee who has generated a previous employer's appreciation, respect, and concern.

The usual recommendations are to canvass local colleges, universities, and technical schools; to set aside a block of time, at least 45 uninterrupted minutes, to interview each candidate; to look for commitment and an ability to work with people; to check references; and to hire the winner. A great theory. It is better than nothing, but just barely.

I never place or scan classified ads, and have never used employment agencies. Perhaps when the business gets multiple employees, it may be worth using these screening mechanisms. Starting out, however, personal contacts are the best way to screen potential employees and find out about them.

The small business ideal is hand-picked people. Hand pick people you know when you run into them. As you are developing the business you may identify someone before you could really justify hiring. That was my case. I identified my present assistant when she was working for someone else. Luckily she was laid off her previous job just as I was ready to hire. She was unemployed for a grand total of half an hour. Similarly, as you come in contact with clients and other businesses, you may identify the perfect employee. Although I have never done it myself, once you make your decision to hire a certain person, go ahead: **Steal 'em**. It's legitimate. We are in business, and business is competitive. You may know, for example, that that person is dissatisfied in the current job. Hiring may not cost more than modifying the working hours. If the potential employee has other than monetary needs, offer the same or a similar salary but change the work load, or other features of the employment, to make it attractive. Don't hesitate to make the offer, but be serious about it. Make up your mind, make your commitment in advance, and then go after the employee you want.

If you can't find employees like this, use personal contacts as much as you can anyway. Contact the faculty of local colleges, universities, and technical schools and ask about promising students. As I said, interviewing for help is not easy and the results are not guaranteed. If you do it, set aside that uninterrupted block of around 45 minutes per interview. Look for commitment, decisiveness, and the ability to work with people. You may choose enthusiasm over experience, although it helps if the employee has a background in the business to start with. Check all the references and verify degrees. If you use an employment application form, have a lawyer review it for compliance with state and federal equal opportunity laws.

Keeping Good Employees

Once you have good employees hang on to them by providing comfortable wages, good working conditions, plenty of responsibility, and the chance for improvement. First, a friendly atmosphere goes a long way to building a desirable work place. If you are a sourpuss, it won't matter how generous a wage you pay. In a two-person shop you are the professional and your employee is the support person. There is not a lot of room to rise unless the employee wants to and you support it by encouraging and subsidizing education, examinations, licensing, and so on. In that case, your employee could become a partner or a colleague. Then you hire someone else to be support staff. At very least, the employee has to perceive that a position with you is better than the one just vacated and offers some potential the other did not.

Most assistants and support staff in this business will be women. Some will be single parents. One major need and concern of single parents is to have adequate health coverage for themselves and their families. It will be one of the major expenses above the hourly wage. Health insurance is probably a given that you should be prepared to provide. I will discuss one option later on. Dental insurance may be important to employees with bad teeth or who have kids with orthodontic needs. If the employee considers it important, you may want to discuss it as a fringe benefit. It could be a bargaining chip in some point of hiring or later employee relations.

The employment contract must provide for sick leave, and you can negotiate whether some sick leave is to be paid and a certain amount unpaid. Sick leave is essential. Employees with small children or other dependents need enough flexibility to take time off without a feeling of jeopardizing their jobs.

Paid vacation can be administered like a bonus. There should be a standard two-week period each year to begin with. Then as the person stays and raises his or her value to you, you can increase it.

We can inform Jonathan [the United States] what are the inevitable consequences of being too fond of glory . . . taxes on everything on earth and the waters under the earth.

—Rev. Sydney Smith (1771-1845)
WORKS, vol i,
Review of Seybert's STATISTICAL
ANNALS OF THE UNITED STATES

All of these benefits can be manipulated and adjusted to fit the situation. It helps to have these and other employee policies written down. Even a small firm can benefit from a written policy manual, even if it is a few sheets stapled together. Both employee and employer should have a copy. There is even software for a ready-made policy manual. It is a little too elaborate but can be tailored to size. Or, a client may have a policy manual you can borrow and crib from. As long as you don't have to reinvent the wheel, use whatever model serves you well. The reason for the manual is not to be inflexible about your relations with your employee but because memory is so unreliable that you could fall into a "you said . . . I said . . ." situation.

The Paperwork

Employees mean volumes of paperwork. Fortunately we are in a business where we can have the employee handle his or her own paperwork. In fact, if you get into payroll accounting, that can be one of the employee's jobs. I try to avoid payroll work, and it is terrific to have someone in the office who can handle my clients' payroll needs while I take care of their other business. Just to cover the subject without going into too much detail, I will list briefly what payroll entails.

When you plan to become an employer contact the IRS for Form SS-4 to get an Employer Identification Number (EIN). Also get W-4 forms for employee tax withholding and, while you are at it, a supply of W-2 forms. Before January 31 of the following year you must send one W-2 to the Social Security Administration, keep one for your records, and give the employee three copies.

You will need to set up a payroll sheet for the employee and comply with all the state and federal laws, rules, and regulations that apply to employers. This means carrying workers' compensation, either through your state or a private insurer, and complying with Occupational Safety and Health Administration (OSHA) regulations, with the Immigration Reform and Control Act (IRCA), and with the Fair Labor Standards Act (FLSA). You will have to pay for unemployment insurance and for half of your employees' Social Security.

- *OSHA*. To maintain safe working conditions, the Occupational Safety and Health Administration, a division of the U.S. Department of Labor, publishes minimum standards for each industry and inspects workplaces. It is highly unlikely an OSHA inspector will ever come calling on a bookkeeping and tax-preparation service, but that is no reason to get careless and invite trouble.

- *IRCA*. You and every employee you hire must fill out an INS Form I-9. The federal Immigration and Naturalization Act permits you to hire only U.S. citizens and aliens who are permitted to work here. For compliance with the Act you must review documents like birth certificates, drivers' licenses, Social Security cards, passports, visas, naturalization papers, and green cards. You must decide whether the documents are genuine and then record the evidence of your compliance on Form I-9. The form's instructions take you through the steps of filling it out. Each employee's Form I-9 must remain in your records for at least three years, or one year after a longer term employee leaves. Contact the nearest INS office or telephone 1-800-777-7700 for publication M274, its *Handbook for Employers*.

- *FLSA*. The Fair Labor Standards Act sets the minimum wage and the standard work week, and determines overtime pay. There is no restriction on anyone over 16 years of age working more than 40 hours a week, but the act requires compensating at time and one half for work exceeding the standard work week. What exceeds the standard work week is fairly complicated. Watch out that this does not become a special problem during the tax season. It is all right for you to work 90 hours a week, but your employee can't unless you pay him or her one and one half times his or her usual pay for the excess.

- *FUTA*. You must also pay federal unemployment tax on each employee and file it with an IRS Form 940 or 940EZ if: (1) you paid $1,500 or more in wages in any quarter of a year or (2) had (a) at least one employee for (b) part of at least one day of (c) 20 different weeks in a year. The tax is calculated on the employee's first $7,000 of wages during the year, and any state unemployment tax is credited to your federal tax liability.

- *FICA*. You pay your portion of your employees' Social Security taxes directly and withhold the employees' equivalent portion from their gross pay. These are reported on Form 941.

- *Workers' Compensation*. All states require employers to carry workers' compensation insurance. The laws vary from state to state, and you should contact your state agency for details. As a sole proprietor you can't cover yourself with workers' compensation, but a partnership or corporation may elect to provide you with coverage as a partner of the partnership or officer of the corporation.

As you may deduce, all of this paperwork is daunting to the average business person and can be a fertile market to cultivate. I don't want to do it any more than the average Joe. I have an assistant who is a whiz, but it still isn't a part of my practice.

In the State of California and many others you are mandated as an employer to pay into State Disability Insurance for your employees unless you are self-insured. The only ones who self-insure are the big utility companies and public entities. Although disability insurance is mandated for employees, you, the boss or entrepreneur are out in the cold. I discussed it earlier under insurance. As you pay into your employees' state mandated fund, think about setting up coverage for yourself.

Medical and dental insurance on employees are worthwhile benefits to consider. In California some employees, especially those who are single parents may be eligible for catastrophic coverage through the Medicare system, whether or not combined with a state program. Usually for these types of coverage the determining factors are the income level and number of dependents.

If your employee is eligible you may consider supplementing that plan by agreeing to pick up the monthly "co-payment" in case the employee must actually use the coverage. The advantage is that you know definitely what the amount of the co-payment will be in any given month, and you can go for long periods when everybody is healthy and incurs no expenses at all. My experience has been that in some months the need might arise to co-pay $50-$60 for a doctor visit, or perhaps less than $100 in any given month.

"It was as true . . . as turnips is. It was as true . . . as taxes is. And nothing's truer than that."

—Charles Dickens (1812-1870)
Mr. Barkis in DAVID COPPERFIELD

Some months go by without any expense at all. Depending on the public coverage available in your state, this may be an option to look into if your employee qualifies. Many government funded plans are in flux at the time of this writing, and the benefits described here may not be available. If they are not, you will have to shop for an insurer on the open market or through your professional association, if you belong to one, to find coverage for your employees and their dependents.

You will want a carrier that provides reliable coverage when you need it at a good rate. The lowest bidder may not be the best provider. Whether you are buying insurance or copier paper, be conscious of cost versus value. Wherever possible, let cost be the secondary consideration. It will do no good to pay cheap health insurance premiums if the company doesn't cover you when you need it or goes bust before you can collect.

You and Your New Assistant

You may think you are the most important person in your shop, but in fact it is very often the person who answers the telephone or sits at the front desk who determines whether you have happy clients and a healthy practice. It isn't enough to be the fastest gun in town on state and federal taxes, able to nail every loophole, and have all manner of experience and skill. You will never get to exercise your talents if your clients get cut off at the telephone or at the front door. They will go away mad, and you will never know why until word gets around to you secondhand. You want to avoid that problem from the outset.

When you hire someone competent, explain how you like things done. Good client relations are less of a problem if you hire somebody who is naturally pleasant, bright, easy to get along with, well-groomed, considerate, and well-mannered in the first place. Then you can deal with the subtleties and nuances of how to answer the telephone, what to say, and how to handle client inquiries.

Never let your employee alienate your clients. Your employee is an extension of you. Use the policy manual to cover this and be sure the employee has memorized the basic rules. Keep those rules simple. They are consideration, politeness, and the ability to keep cool when the client is upset. When clients are upset they are liable to say all kinds of things they don't mean. When you, the professional, cause the client grief, the client is going to unload on the first person who answers the phone. You need to let your assistant know that, if the client is upset and are berating him or her, it is not personal and has nothing to do with the employee, but has to do with you.

I will not tolerate clients' abuse, however, of me or my assistant. The client may be entitled to be upset, and my responsibility as the boss and professional is to try to understand the problem and solve it. But being upset does not give the client the right to be abusive to me or my assistant. You must be willing to support your assistant and back him or her up and take the heat. You are in charge, and the buck stops with you. You are in charge, AREN'T YOU?

The secretary for a lawyer in our town, call him Smith, tells abusive clients, "you can't talk to Mr. Smith unless you are nice to Mr. Smith's secretary." Well, it shouldn't come to that. Unfortunately every upset client is so different there is no pat response, and you have to handle every situation as it comes up. The main points are (1) to keep your cool although the client may be getting a little out of control, and (2) to take the heat off your assistant as quickly as you can.

Personnel Matters

Some people advise keeping notes on discussions with employees about all personnel matters. I feel uncomfortable with that in a small business like mine. It has its value, and you can save a lot of grief if at the time of the conversation you make a permanent record and put it in a file. Sometimes copying and filing a simple note to the employee is all you need. Don't be a sneak. Memory is never what we'd like it to be. All you need is a written reminder.

Firing is a lot harder than hiring. If you do a good job of hiring you may never have to do it. If you do, fire as carefully as you hired. Lawyers have found out about lawsuits for wrongful termination, and even small employers can face nasty, expensive litigation. Before firing someone, be sure that you have a good reason to do it, that it is clear you hired the employee for an "at will" position, and that you never made any promises or suggestions about tenure with the company. If you have to fire a long-time employee, meeting these standards gets very difficult. You may want to see *your* lawyer first.

From the Annals of Internal Revenue

In 1937, a period of activist government during the Great Depression, the total dollar amount of internal revenue began to rise sharply. From 1922 to 1941 tax collection rose from $1.6 billion to $7.4 billion. With World War II, taxes rose even faster, with collection in 1945 at $45 billion. As in World War I, the total $153 billion in taxes collected in World War II did not cover the war's cost. Public debt stood at $280 billion at the war's end, six times what it had been just before the attack on Pearl Harbor.

The first of three significant wartime changes came with the adoption in 1941 of short-form return. Next came the withholding of taxes in 1943, and in 1944 the standard deduction. Withholding did not change existing rates, but a Victory Tax on personal incomes was added in 1943. The flurry of other taxes that arose during the war prompted President Roosevelt to propose tax simplification in his budget message to Congress in 1944. The result was the Individual Income Tax Act of 1944. This law created a uniform $500 personal exemption and replaced the Victory Tax with a new tax on net income. It also provided for a standard deduction of 10 percent and relieved millions of taxpayers of having to file declarations of estimated tax.

Following World War II, Congress again proposed tax cuts, and President Truman signed a $9 billion relief bill that reduced individual and corporate tax rates and removed 12 million people from the tax rolls. Congress cut taxes again in 1948, this time over President Truman's veto, raised the personal exemption to $600 and let married couples file joint returns.

On July 9, 1953, following Truman's 1953 reorganization plan which replaced the patronage system with career service, President Eisenhower changed the agency's name from the Bureau of Internal Revenue to the Internal Revenue Service, in part to focus on its function as a service to taxpayers.

*Just remember when investi-
gating pension plans that, if
you are going to cover yourself, you will also have to
cover your employees.*

12

Retirement Options

"**P**ENSION plans," as a generic term, usually refer to qualified plans available to other than sole-proprietorship entities, like small corporations and partnerships. In days gone by it was possible to overload a pension plan in employer's favor, sometimes at the employee's expense. With the advent of ERISA and other regulatory schemes, however, that is no longer permissible.

Even if not subject to the strictures of ERISA, practitioners should examine retirement preferences in terms, not only of funding their own retirement plans, but also as to what retirement benefits to provide for their employees. This is not just a matter of good employment practice. The plans' rules and regulations are very strict about not excluding employees and against unduly in favoring the principal—you. To cover the details of plan options and keep them mercifully short, this chapter offers only a few broad strokes to outline the major plan options and provides a table describing the features of each.

Keogh Plans

Keogh Plans are specifically designed for the self-employed, those who are not incorporated or in partnership but are sole proprietors. Since this book has emphasized the sole proprietor, and since Keoghs provide for employee participation, it is worth considering them seriously as investment vehicles. Keoghs also offer very liberal participation rules for employees.

Briefly, it permits the individual owner/participant to put away in the neighborhood of 15 percent (currently it is 13.0435%) of net self-employment income, that is, all income left over after deducting expenses but before calculating taxes. They differ from more familiar plans like Individual Retirement Accounts (IRAs) by letting you deposit a greater amount of money.

Today the upper limit of Keoghs is 13.0435 percent of net self-employment income up to a maximum of $30,000 annually. There is also a provision that lets the individual incur an amount of Keogh deduction above 20 percent by incorporating what is called a "defined benefit" portion. While this increases the percentage of deductible income, the percentage that falls under the defined benefit portion also has a mandatory funding requirement. The potential problem with it is that whether or not you are making a profit, you may still have to fund the defined benefit part of the pension plan.

Profit sharing is a variation on a retirement plan that, again, relates not to a sole proprietorship but to small corporations or partnerships. Profit sharing allows building more flexibility into it, because it will depend on whether or not you are making a profit. The lower the profits, the lower the dollar amount of the contribution required, although the percentage of contribution stays the same.

The rules and regulations vary somewhat for different kinds of retirement plans, but all include a provision—some of them very liberal—for covering employees. Just remember when investigating these plans that, if you are going to cover yourself, you will also have to cover your employees. The table outlining the major features of different plans shown here is from IRS Publication 560.

Social Security

Social Security is, of course, a mandatory payment. As the employer, you are required to pay half the Social Security contribution, and the employee is mandated to pay the other half. If you are self-employed, you are obliged to pay what is called Self Employment Tax, which is simply a self-employed person's version of Social Security. You get to pay both halves of the mandatory amount. Currently it approximates 15 percent of profits or self-employment income. Self Employment Tax is

Table of Key Retirement Plan Rules

Type of Plan	Last Date for Contribution	Maximum Contribution			Time Limit to Begin Distributions[1]
IRA	Due date of income tax return (excluding extensions)	Smaller of $2,000 or taxable compensation			April 1 of year after reaching age 70½
SEP-IRA	Due date of employer's return (Plus extensions)	Smaller of $30,000 or 15%[2] of participant's taxable compensation[3]			April 1 of year after reaching age 70½
Keogh		**Defined Contribution Plans**			
			Employee	**Self-Employed**	
	Due date of employer's return (plus extensions). (To make contributions for a year to a new plan, the plan must be set up by the last day of the employer's tax year.)		Money Purchase: Smaller of $30,000 or 25% employee's taxable compensation	Money Purchase: Smaller of $30,000 or 20% of self-employed participant's compensation[4]	April 1 of year after reaching age 70½ before 1988, in which case the distributions must begin by the year of retirement.
		Defined Benefit Plans			
		Amount needed to provide an annual retirement benefit no larger than the smaller of $118,800 or 100% of the participant's average taxable compensation for the highest 3 consecutive years			

1. Distributions of at least the required minimum amount must be made each year if the entire balance is not distributed.
2. 13.0435% of the self-employed participant's taxable compensation before adjustment for this contribution.
3. Contributions are made to each participant's IRA (SEP-IRA) including that of any self-employed participant.
4. Compensation is before adjustment for this contribution.

a mandatory tax above any income tax that is due, and it is an additional burden for the self-employed person.

Another important consideration about Social Security and its role in a retirement plan is that as an employer you can integrate your employees' pension or other retirement plans with their Social Security. Thus, within certain guidelines you are relieved of making double contributions to the retirement plan. Retirement plan contributions will take account of those you already made to Social Security, thereby reducing the dollar amount needed for whatever form of employee retirement plan you select.

Annuities, Stocks, Real Estate, Precious Metals, Etc.

Annuities fall into either a fixed or variable category. Fixed annuities are, as the name implies, a specified interest rate paid, depending on the contract and the principal paid is guaranteed so that there will be no fluctuation in principal payments. If you invest $1,000, that $1,000 is guaranteed. It is not guaranteed by any branch of the federal government, but by the contracting insurance company. You must be concerned, of course, about the soundness of the company with which you are doing business. The contracts are usually subject to some sort of minimum interest rate, usually in the neighborhood of three to four percent (3% to 4%), which establishes a floor below which payments on the contract will not decline.

They are now offered with indexing to a 10-year Treasury Bill or some other security, also with an established floor, that does not lock you into a specified rate when interest rates are rising. Usually once a year or so the provider will adjust the rate to reflect this indexing to the Treasury Bill, so that you may expect your payback on the annuity to increase when rates rise. Conversely, when rates decline the interest on your annuity will also decline, but it will not fall below the base amount.

The variable annuity is a mutual fund wrapped in an annuity contract. Its advantage is that growth in the underlying investment is tax-deferred until you withdraw it. Over time the rates of return on variables are usually higher than on fixed rates. If you don't withdraw it during your lifetime, however, it benefits only your heirs or the state.

A major consideration for both types of annuities is that, while contributions are made to them with "after-tax dollars," there is no limit on how much you may contribute. Therefore, a sole practitioner willing to supplement another existing pension or Keogh plan may want to consider making after-tax contributions into an annuity to enjoy its tax deferred build-up.

A portfolio of stocks, bonds, and mutual funds is another option. These may be held in a pension plan and referred to as a "qualified plan." Real estate, other than what is available as a Real Estate Investment Trust (REIT), normally cannot be held in a pension plan. Art, antiques, precious metals, and so on are specifically barred from inclusion in qualified retirement plans. You may want to acquire any or all of them, however, with after-tax dollars as part of an overall investment strategy; but don't neglect to set up the basic plan first.

I saw my business as one that needed vertical integration. To prepare winning tax returns for your client you have to work back along a series of events to get in on the planning stage.

13

Diversifying

THE real pleasure of reaching the point where you can turn over a lot of the work you don't want to do to somebody else is the time it gives you to focus on work you like and to consider how to expand the practice and extend it into allied services. There is one prerequisite.

Having found good people, you must give them responsibility. Delegating responsibility within your business relates in some degree to personal security. There are people who simply cannot let go, who must keep control of every part of every detail. It is a poor way to run things. If you have employees, you have to let them do their job. That is what you hired them for. If you won't, you shouldn't have hired them, because you aren't prepared to grow with them. If you make the commitment to delegate responsibility, and let the business grow and diversify, it can increase your potential for profit and help protect against the inevitable downturns in the business cycle.

Diversification as Self Defense

When you consider diversifying be wary of spreading your interest and attention too thin. On the other hand, you should know that some companion enterprises arise naturally out of the business. My experience early on was that people don't like to pay taxes and their tendency to "shoot the messenger" is an occupational hazard for tax preparers. I would find myself doing a return that required horrendous penalties and surcharges because of decisions the client had made long before I got involved. In March or April, when I gave the client the bad news about his or her decisions, that client would then be unhappy *with me*. Clients have accused me of incompetence, of making mistakes, of all kinds of things, when in fact they failed to plan ahead adequately. My response, and it may well be yours, was to move from tax preparation and record-keeping alone into financial planning and investments.

These can be very gainfully integrated into the business. I moved one step back from tax preparation and sat down with clients to map out strategies for diversifying assets, reducing taxes, and so forth. I would then send the client down to the friendly brokerage house to execute our plan. By the time the brokers got done with my client, my careful plans were a shambles. The client would come back just before tax season having done nothing I suggested. The super-broker down at the big-name securities firm, motivated by a desire for a commission, usually convinced the client to do something else entirely, and the client's tax position would be no better than before.

Over and over again courts have said that there is nothing sinister in arranging one's affairs to keep taxes as low as possible. Everybody does so, rich or poor; and all do right, for nobody owes any public duty to pay more than the law demands.

—Judge Learned Hand (1872-1961)

Gradually, I saw my business as one that needed vertical integration. Tax preparation is the end result of a whole series of decisions and events that take place sometime in the past. To prepare winning tax returns for your client, you have to work back along that series of events to get in on the planning stage. As a result I have extended the range of my services in order to implement the tax plan through stock and insurance brokerage services that I recommended in the planning phase.

Securities and Insurance Brokerage

It is very easy to combine record keeping and tax preparation, with tax planning, and investment and insurance product development or offerings. You can create an integrated package that ultimately will benefit the client, reduce frustration, and provide you with more than one profit center. It can also mean prosperous and resilient clients. The planning process calls for a fee structure to take account of the combined services offered. You will already have fee schedules for bookkeeping and tax preparation, and if you are licensed to provide a brokerage service for stocks and insurance, you can be entitled to the commissions these products generate.

You must be very careful to make full disclosure to the client when you jump from fees for services to commissions for sales. So a rigorous policy that avoids double-billing the client is critical to this combination of services. That is, if you develop a financial plan, it is a stand-alone entity that the client can shop around to implement. You can inform the client of the option to implement the plan through you, with the result that you will receive commissions.

If the client does choose to invest through me, my policy, which I recommend, is to credit the client for any commissions. If the client pays for the plan and takes it to Merrill Lynch or elsewhere, I am paid for my time to develop the plan. If the client chooses to follow my investment advice and implement it through me, I credit the account with the commissions I receive. It goes a long way toward establishing credibility and an understanding in the clients that my primary motivation is their welfare as opposed to whatever commissions I might generate from any investment I recommended. It avoids a conflict of interest. I have the system spelled out in the engagement letter detailing the process, which I have the client sign. The full letter is set forth in the Appendix.

This kind of extension into sideline or companion businesses fits right in. It is the old "one stop shopping" idea. I am a big fan of that.

If you wish to pursue stock brokerage you would get a Series 7 License from the National Association of Securities Dealers (NASD). Once licensed you would affiliate with a reputable national broker/dealer, and do business through it. The major "wire houses" like Merrill-Lynch require their brokers to deal entirely in stock transactions, but smaller firms will accommodate brokers who deal in other than stock.

The NASD is a self-regulating body designated by Congress to monitor the integrity of the over-the-counter (OTC) market and the ethics of brokers and dealers who trade in its stocks. The NASD's brokerage courses are available by correspondence or, if you live in an urban area, directly from a major brokerage firm. An insurance license is issued by the department or commission of the state you live in. In California it is the Department of Insurance.

Property Exchange Facilitator

Another companion business that I have not yet engaged in is to be a facilitator for Internal Revenue Code Section 1031 tax-deferred real property exchanges. The nearest such services for my community are available only in a medium-sized city, about 75 miles southwest of us. The techniques for facilitating such an exchange of property would mesh nicely with the rest of your business. This service is most promising in a rural area like mine, where highly specialized facilitator firms rarely set up offices. Usually an attorney or real estate broker will organize the exchange, but the parties need a disinterested third party—the facilitator—as a stakeholder to keep cash receipts out of the exchangers' hands. The tax code and regulations themselves are the ultimate authority for conducting such an exchange; however, an excellent text to consult on 1031 exchanges is *Real Estate Exchange and Acquisition Techniques*, by William T. Tappan, Jr.

Private Conservatorships

Another peripheral service I do provide is that of a private, professional conservator. To my knowledge, I am the only one in my county. The work involves money and asset management, under the direct supervision of a court of law, to maintain the assets and provide for the needs of a person who may be incompetent because of age or disability. It does not afford an opportunity to sell products or make commissions, as that would cause a conflict of interest. You can, however, charge an hourly fee for managing the estate's assets, and that can be very remunerative. I have a two-tier fee structure, in which I charge so much per hour for my assistant's clerical help and a lower professional fee of my own for conservatorship work. This can become a comfortable sideline. It branches off into estate administration if the conservatee dies intestate. It is an area of business that makes good use of your knowledge of record keeping, asset management, and tax planning. Amazingly, it does not require a special license. Anybody can do it, but you have an advantage with your specialized tax knowledge and the reputation you will be building in the business community.

Consumer Credit Counseling

Even your most basic skills are a marketable asset. A bankruptcy lawyer I know told me recently that filing for a Chapter 7 or 13 bankruptcy has such a calamitous effect on personal credit records that he usually advises potential clients to investigate consumer credit counseling first and use bankruptcy only as a last resort.

Independently of that lawyer's advice, I have developed consumer credit counseling as an added service. Many people who grew up in the recent prosperity acquired a peculiar idea of thrift, if they ever had one. Now in the lean 1990s many of them are having trouble managing past debt. Getting their finances in order meshes nicely with a full-service bookkeeping business.

For some of my debt-counseling clients the choice had been no less than to bring their finances to me or file a petition in bankruptcy. What I do is try to head off bankruptcy and revive their economic lives. I contact their creditors and attempt to work out a payment schedule that suits all parties. By the time I step in, most creditors are delighted at the prospect of getting any money at all, so arranging a payment plan is usually fairly straightforward. Occasionally, a large creditor like a bank or major department store is inflexible and the only solution is to resort to the bankruptcy trustee. Usually, however, I can work out a plan. It has gotten a little easier, because I find myself working with the same creditors over and over again, and we have begun to know and trust one another.

To make the plan work, I need to get all the creditors in on it. If one creditor turns down a deferred pay-back, then sues for the entire balance and wins a judgment against the client, bankruptcy is usually the only recourse. If you overlook a creditor, it may look like everyone is being paid off, until the neglected creditor files a lawsuit for principal, back interest, and costs. The result can be devastating to the clients and very embarrassing for the planner. At least have the client prepare the list of creditors and sign a statement that it contains all of them.

Essentially, a consumer credit counseling plan amounts to putting both clients and creditors on an allowance. We destroy the clients' credit cards. They send me their paychecks, and I pay all their bills and give them a certain amount of money after the creditors are paid. It is critical to prevent the clients from incurring new debt. If they start building it up again, they will frustrate the plan.

I charge an hourly fee for setting up and administering the plan. In time, as delinquent bills are paid off and by agreement with my clients, I use the extra money to set up retirement and savings accounts for them. The response I get has been surprising. Clients have told me that putting their finances into my hands is like having a cloud lifted, and for the first time in their lives they do not have money worries and are actually saving for their future. It can be a gratifying experience.

This is a service that target advertising can help build. Some large city newspapers have classified-ad sections for bankruptcy help and credit counseling. If you live in a small town, look over your local paper for a likely spot. Don't neglect free weekly shoppers like the *Penny Saver*. Some people read them cover to cover for bargains. You may also spot people from your tax-preparation service who can use the services. Offering it to clients in the privacy of your office preserves the confidentiality that such a service merits. See the Appendix for the forms I use.

Payroll

Payroll can also be an element of the bookkeeping side of the business. It is usually part of doing a quarterly statement or the like for a bookkeeping client. A firm can specialize strictly in payroll. It is an area I have not gotten into. There is a good deal of it available. It is also very tedious work, the reason I don't do it. In order to supervise the payroll process, you need a comprehensive understanding of it. I don't have such knowledge and frankly I don't want it. Other people in the business may find that payroll and other activities that I do not relish dovetail very neatly with their practices. That makes it a big, wide, wonderful market.

Next Two Pages:

Tax year 1982 saw the introduction of the Form 1040EZ (shown here) for single taxpayers. The Service's recent efforts at ease of tax payment have included electronic filing and Form 1040-TEL, which introduced telephone filing in 1996. Further changes will depend on how Congress decides to alter the income tax in the future.

Department of the Treasury — Internal Revenue Service

Form 1040EZ Income Tax Return for

1982

Single filers with no dependents ∞

OMB No. 1545-0675

Instructions are on the back of this form.
Tax Table is in the 1040EZ and 1040A Tax Package.

Name and address

Use the IRS mailing label. If you don't have a label, print or type:

Name (first, initial, last) | Social security number

Present home address

City, town or post office, State, and ZIP code

Presidential Election Campaign Fund
Check this box ☐ if you want $1 of your tax to go to this fund.

Figure your tax

Attach Copy B of Forms W-2 here

1 Wages, salaries, and tips. Attach your W-2 form(s).   1

2 Interest income of $400 or less. If more than $400, you cannot use Form 1040EZ.   2

3 Add line 1 and line 2. This is your **adjusted gross income.**   3

4 Allowable part of your charitable contributions. Complete the worksheet on page 18. Do not write more than $25.   4

5 Subtract line 4 from line 3.   5

6 Amount of your personal exemption.   6   1,000.00

7 Subtract line 6 from line 5. This is your **taxable income.**   7

8 Enter your Federal income tax withheld. This is shown on your W-2 form(s).   8

9 Use the tax table on pages 26-31 to find the tax on your taxable income on line 7.   9

Refund or amount you owe

Attach tax payment here

10 If line 8 is larger than line 9, subtract line 9 from line 8. Enter the amount of your **refund.**   10

11 If line 9 is larger than line 8, subtract line 8 from line 9. Enter the **amount you owe.** Attach check or money order for the full amount payable to "Internal Revenue Service."   11

Sign your return

I have read this return. Under penalties of perjury, I declare that to the best of my knowledge and belief, the return is correct and complete.

Your signature   Date

X

For **Privacy Act and Paperwork Reduction Act Notice, see page 34.**

1982   Instructions for Form 1040EZ

You can use this form if:	You cannot use this form if:
• Your filing status is single	• Your filing status is other than single
• You do not claim exemptions for being 65 or over. OR for being blind	• You claim exemptions for being 65 or over. OR for being blind
• You do not claim any dependents	• You claim any dependents
• Your taxable income is less than $50,000	• Your taxable income is $50,000 or more
• You had only wages, salaries, and tips and you had interest income of $400 or less	• You had income other than wages and interest income. OR you had interest of over $400 or any interest from an All-Savers Certificate
• You had no dividend income	• You had dividend income

If you can't use this form, you must use Form 1040A or 1040 instead. See pages 4 through 6.
If you are uncertain about your filing status, dependents, or exemptions, read the step-by-step instructions for Form 1040A that begin on page 6.

Completing your return

Name and address
Use the mailing label from the back cover of the instruction booklet. Correct any errors right on the label. But don't place the label on your return until you have completed it. If you don't have a label, print or type the information in the spaces provided. If you don't have a social security number, see page 7.

Presidential election campaign fund
This fund was established by Congress to help pay campaign costs of candidates running for President. You may have one of your tax dollars go to this fund by checking the box.

Figure your tax
Line 1. Write on line 1 the total amount you received in wages, salaries, and tips from all employers.

Your employer should have reported your income on a 1982 wage statement, Form W-2. If you don't receive your W-2 form by February 15, contact your local IRS office. Attach W-2 form(s) to your return.

Line 2. Write on line 2 the total interest income you received from all sources, such as banks, savings and loans, credit unions, and other institutions with which you deposit money. You should receive an interest statement (usually Form 1099-INT) from each institution that paid you interest.

You cannot use Form 1040EZ if your total interest income is over $400 or you received interest income from an All-Savers Certificate.

Line 4. You can deduct 25% of what you gave to qualified charitable organizations in 1982. But if you gave $100 or more, you can't deduct more than $25. Complete the worksheet on page 18 to figure your deduction, and write the amount on line 4.

Line 6. Every taxpayer is entitled to one $1,000 personal exemption. If you are also entitled to additional exemptions for being 65 or over, for blindness, for your spouse, or for your dependent children or other dependents, you cannot use this form. You must use Form 1040A or Form 1040.

Line 8. Write the amount of Federal income tax withheld, as shown on your 1982 W-2 form(s). If you had two or more employers and had total wages of over $32,400, see page 19. If you want IRS to figure your tax for you, complete lines 1 through 8, sign, and date your return. If you want to figure your own tax, continue with these instructions.

Line 9. Use the amount on line 7 to find your tax in the tax table on pages 26-31. Be sure to use the column in the tax table for single taxpayers. Write the amount of tax on line 9.

Refund or amount you owe
Line 10. Compare line 8 with line 9. If line 8 is larger than line 9, you are entitled to a refund. Subtract line 9 from line 8, and write the result on line 10.

Line 11. If line 9 is larger than line 8, you owe more tax. Subtract line 8 from line 9, and write the result on line 11. Attach your check or money order for the full amount. Write your social security number and "1982 Form 1040EZ" on your payment.

Sign your return
You must sign and date your return. If you pay someone to prepare your return, that person must also sign it below the space for your signature and supply the other information required by IRS. See page 22.

Mailing your return
Your return is due by April 15, 1983. Use the addressed envelope that came with the instruction booklet. If you don't have an addressed envelope, see page 25 for the correct address.

Diversification as a Recession Strategy

One good thing about being in the tax-preparation business is that, regardless of the economy, people have to file tax returns. At this point I will interject a little philosophy. Owing largely to the extreme complexity and onerous burden of tax law and its interpretation, many people have decided to drop out of the system. The system got worse from about 1980 onward. Congress has messed around with the tax laws so often and in such extreme ways—practically reinventing it in 1986—that more and more taxpayers have simply gone off the record by going underground and not filing tax returns.

The IRS estimates that roughly 10 million taxpayers fail to file a tax return in any year, regardless of the state of the economy. My own experience is that non-filing is worse when the economy experiences a downturn. While it is true, theoretically, that everybody has to file a tax return and the tax-preparation business should stay recession-proof, you can expect to lose some clients in periods of severe economic stress. Not only tax preparation and bookkeeping fall off, but so do financial planning and advising, along with investment and insurance brokerage. In down times like that you emphasize the parts of the business that are still viable and draw back on those that atrophy until the economy revives.

It is just another argument for diversifying profit centers and having those other things available to carry you over. Know the basics but diversify. If you restrict your business to income tax alone or bookkeeping alone, or even both, there may some very lean times coming up. You need to be sure how to do these, but I would not hesitate to diversify into offering services as a facilitator or a private professional conservator. Consumer credit counseling may also do well in bad economic times. I would not diversify into payroll, but someone else may be very happy with payroll.

It is a poor idea to lower prices during a recession when you can increase the amount of services offered at the same price. Try adding services as way to create value and show clients that you are in their corner. Good times or bad, be sensitive of the client's financial condition. If they are pinched because of the general downturn in business, you should know them well enough to know that when times improve they will be good clients and that when times are bad you can be supportive by offering them more services at the same price. Offer things that will help them through the bad times they are experiencing. You might even have to balance that with getting paid, so do it as long as you are sensible about it.

Diversification and the Client

To diversify successfully, if at all, you need to understand clients' emotions about money; for most people these are second in sensitivity only to their feelings about the state of their health. Like a family doctor, a financial advisor may become privy to some of the most intimate details of clients' lives. Being aware of their sensitivity is basic to maintaining good client relations but it is particularly relevant to diversifying. A confidential relationship based on doing a client's taxes or books will not necessarily permit extending it into other services.

To become a financial advisor you must first win the client's absolute trust and confidence. Even then, don't be disappointed if a client declines your offer of services. And don't be surprised if, in the extreme case, a client perceives the mere mention of other financial services as a threat and leaves. Upsetting as a sudden departure may be when it happens, my experience is that the vast majority of clients appreciate an honest offer of assistance in other areas of their financial lives. Getting clients to accept your offers, however, means developing that sixth sense and approaching each client individually.

A Philosophy for Growth

How fast and far you let the business grow is a matter of personal preference. If you want to maintain a small, comfortable practice, it means setting a limit to how much business to take in. If you want to build an empire or conglomerate, you are in a different category. It calls for planning and delegation on a much greater scale than you will find outlined here. Either way, the point is to avoid letting the business grow faster than you can manage it. To keep it under control, you should have a business plan, which is the subject of this book's next and final chapter.

*The plan's two purposes are:
internal—to get yourself organized and see how you are
doing; and external—to let
potential lenders understand
the business clearly.*

14

Business Plans

Now that you have all the information in this book under your hat, you should be better prepared to construct and draft a business plan. I saved this for last because at this point we should be talking the same language, or near enough. I have regaled you with my experiences and warned of the pitfalls awaiting a bookkeeper/tax preparer. Armed with a little extra knowledge from this book and some advice on where to find market data, you can turn your thoughts to planning your business.

Why You Plan the Business

There is a sizable body of literature and computer software dealing with business plans. Very little of it is any good. That's a pity, because an entrepreneur should have a solid plan before committing any resources to a new venture. A business plan on its simplest level is a general idea going into the business about how much revenue and net income you need, and how much business it will take to generate the revenue. The plan becomes more complex—and valuable—as you refine, break out, and substantiate your idea.

There are several good reasons for having a business plan. One is to help define goals and assumptions more clearly. It is a way to take stock of personal and financial assets, to analyze the market, and to weigh the risks and potential rewards. A business plan is that last extra step toward insuring the new venture's success. It can provide a yardstick on which to measure its progress and to make adjustments—in the business and the yardstick. In addition, potential funding sources will require a clearly drafted business plan before extending credit to the business. The plan's two purposes, therefore, are *internal*—to get yourself organized and see how you are doing—and *external*—to let potential lenders understand the business clearly.

I learned this at least by my experiment: that if one advances confidently in the direction of his dreams, and endeavors to live that life which he has imagined, he will meet with a success unexpected in common hours. . . . If you have built castles in the air, your work need not be lost; that is where they should be. Now put the foundations under them.

—Henry David Thoreau (1817-1862)
WALDEN

The plan can help to avoid common business traps, like incurring too much debt to expand the business, overextending credit to build the client base, and taking on too much work. The plan provides a sense of the business's financial capacity as it grows, and can show how much business is enough. For example, it is better to do less work well and promptly than to overload yourself. Overload can irritate clients by delaying the work and lowering its quality. If you find this happening, it means there is plenty of work to do, but that you have to do it effectively and efficiently. If you have a plan to refer to, it may reveal that this is where you buy a needed piece of equipment or hire an assistant. On a personal level you need to understand clearly when overextension and overload begin to degrade the quality of your life.

On the external level, you may need financing at some point from banks or private investors. Whether they know you or not, they will need a business plan to understand your enterprise as you understand it. You want to make sure that everyone, including you, recognizes the assumptions of risk and reward inherent in your venture.

Help for Drafting the Plan

Drafting a business plan is a lot of work and not all of it is fun. If you have a business plan that outlines what you want and how to go after it, however, you will spend less time spinning your wheels and going nowhere. A whole industry has sprung up almost like that for résumés to serve the need to draft business plans. They all offer similar services, but like every industry a few providers are excellent, the rest are not. One source I recommend is David H. Bangs' *Business Planning Guide*. I think it provides the best discussion of arranging all the disorganized thoughts about your business into one concise, careful statement.

In California residents of every city and town have access to a quasi-governmental entity, usually at the county level, called a Community Development Commission (CDC), Small Business Development Center (SBDC), or Department, or the like. Typically the agency has people on its payroll who can teach how to write a business plan. In some instances, they will sit down with you, brainstorm the project, and refine your information to produce a usable document. It wouldn't hurt to see if there is a similar service in your state.

Writing down your plan is the best way for you, and the only way for others, to spot its flaws. You will want to know about and correct the venture's flaws before you invest capital or time in it. As counseled in the Bible, "Thou shalt read, mark, and inwardly digest." That is, read the market, the statistical guides, the telephone directory; survey established businesses. Mark with the mechanical work of writing down your hard-won information. Then inwardly digest it as you edit your final draft. This is a remarkably educational exercise. It isn't easy but it is invaluable. It will be the most rewarding investment of time and effort you will do over the entire course of your new venture. If you did the community research set forth in Chapter 6, you have a good idea what the market is. At least you should have talked informally to other practitioners and community leaders. It does take a long time, but you may be spending two years getting experience from an established practitioner. Use that time to plan your business. An old friend once wrote advising never to start vast projects with half vast ideas. I only appreciated what he meant when I told it to someone else.

Pieces of the Plan

First the plan needs basic data like your name, address, telephone number, location, and the name of the business. Then it must explain what the business will do and give a focused statement of its purpose, a summary of its objectives, how the business will work, and its prospects for success in the proposed market. It must include equipment lists and prices, and advertising and promotional plans. It must provide a personal financial statement and your financial plans for the business. It must carefully detail the competition, who you are, and what your qualifications are.

Things to consider are: "How much money do you need to get the business going?" "How much money do you need to live on?" "How many hours do you anticipate putting into the business?" "How realistic are your goals?"

You need a feeling for the local market for your services and what your share of it can be. You need to identify who your primary competitors are and how you can compete with them or create an alternative market niche that others in the same market do not serve.

The business's financial plan should include projected financial statements, including potential revenues and expense forecasts, with a break-even analysis and targeted financial statements over a relative period (three months, six months, a year). It can also be incorporated into a five-year plan or goal. As noted, the checklists and spreadsheets in the Appendix may help here. Calculate the method and costs of expanding at various stages as nearly as you can. Also tentatively note projected equipment acquisitions and staff increases at each stage, if only for your own use.

Personal information about your educational background, qualifications, work experience, and your personal financial disclosure of assets and liabilities, may include two or three years of prior tax returns. Finally, credit any management assistance or preparation assistance you received to develop the plan. It's a big job, but necessary and within your capabilities.

You can't anticipate or insure against everything that will happen over the course of your business life, but you might hypothesize a casualty loss of a certain magnitude and how you would overcome it. For example, I had a partner who, unknown to me (although I had begun to suspect) and for reasons that are unimportant now, incurred debts that drained the business of thousands of dollars. When I finally discovered the losses, my share of the partnership liabilities amounted to nearly $200,000. I lost everything, my house, my car, the business.

Well, what are the alternatives in a case like this? Even if you project say, a $20,000 loss, you might have to take a bigger hit than anticipated.

So don't limit your possible responses. Would you have enough cash to pay off creditors? Could you get a loan to shore up your finances? Is Chapter 11 reorganization a choice? My decision was to close the business, pay off what I could, leave town, and start working at my current business—solo—to pay off the rest. I didn't go into bankruptcy, and it is all behind me now. But that was just my way of handling it.

There are always warning signs when someone closely involved in your life or work begins to develop a personal problem that can injure the business. When you spot or suspect the symptoms, face the problem right away. The lesson—which I learned the hard way—is to head off little troubles that can grow into mighty disasters and to try to allow for damage control in case the worst happens and proves to be worse than you expected. Finally, if things begin to crash around your ears despite your best efforts, maintaining professional integrity among the ruins means responding in a way that is least harmful to the others involved. Beyond that, every problem is unique, and resolving it is up to you and the options available.

Putting the Plan in Perspective

There are a few general rules, call them attitudes, to keep in mind when drafting a business plan. First is that net profit is the best measure of a plan's success. Without it you won't be in business very long. But it is not the only measure. Do not forget the quality of life. It makes no sense to beat yourself to death making a lot of money if you do not get to enjoy any of it.

Second, long range planning pays off. This is true not only of how you start a business, or five or ten years down the road, but of how you are going to finish it. Even at the very beginning you must think of that. A business plan should be drafted with an entry and exit strategy as part of the whole. Every business has a life expectancy, roughly equivalent to your own working life expectancy. As with all things related to investments in business, they are always easy to get into and sometimes extremely difficult to get out of. Plan ahead for it.

Say I have built a practice successfully and I come to a time when I will have to turn it over to somebody else by selling it, or closing it down. The most reasonable strategy, unless you are creating a family business that you expect a child or niece or nephew to take over, is to sell the practice to a younger, rising practitioner. Toward that end you must consider how you present the business's cash flow, profit and liabilities, balance sheet, and income statement.

A lot of clients who operate small businesses are immediately concerned with avoidance of taxation, avoidance of including employees in their retirement plan, and so forth. So for years their tax return will show, in a way that is almost fraudulent (yes, it does happen), that they are barely squeaking by. But the trap that this lays is that somewhere down the line, that same client will want to qualify for a loan to buy a house or car, and if the last three years of tax returns show an income of $432 for each year, it would take a miracle to convince a bank to lend. The moral in this applies not only to clients but to the practice itself. Why would anyone in his or her right mind pay what you think the business is worth in order to net $432 per year? It is better to pay your taxes and show legitimate, strong financials, because when it is time to sell the business the buyer will be looking at these numbers.

As part of the whole idea of an exit strategy, you will have to demonstrate that you have a desirable practice to buy in order to make a profitable and graceful exit from the business. The way to do that is to show your profits legitimately and pay the taxes on them. That's just the way it is.

Final Considerations

Don't stagnate. Remember a plan is not carved in stone. You must revisit, revise, and modify it as unforeseen events come up.

Depending on professional designations, continuing education may be mandatory. If you are a CPA, the institute will erase your ticket if you don't keep up. Even if you are not required to continue your education, doing so will make your services more valuable to your clients. It is a wise investment.

Finally, if you are not having any fun, you are not doing yourself or your loved ones any good at all. So keep the following in mind and leave a little air in the plan. You have to manage the daily interruptions as best you can. These are telephone calls from sales people and the inevitable breakdowns of equipment and communication that thwart our best laid schemes. Don't let them become overwhelming and cause you to overlook the essentials like bill-paying that you need to take care of on a daily or monthly basis. Don't get lost in the daily grind, either. One advantage of a business plan is to establish these things and have them written down so that you can look them up when you think you are being distracted by everything at once. Don't forget that even the boss needs a vacation. If you don't consider it realistic, reasonable, or healthy for the other guy to work 80 or 100 hours a week, then it isn't for you either. You will need to schedule time off and vacations not only for your own sanity but to keep peace in the family as well. You will also serve your clients better and do better in your business. If you burn yourself out, you lose and your clients lose.

Once you have planned everything and begun to follow your road map, how will you know whether it is all working the way it is supposed to? Because, like me, you should be having a great time at it.

Appendix

FURTHER READING

Bangs, David H., Jr., *Business Planning Guide* (Dover, NH, 6th Rev. Ed., 1992, Upstart Publishing Co.).

Bly, Robert W., *Selling Your Services: Proven Strategies for Getting Clients to Hire Your Firm* (New York, 1991, Henry Holt & Co.).

Brodsky, Bart, and Janet Geis, *Finding Your Niche—Marketing Your Professional Service* (Berkeley, CA, 1992, Community Resource Institute Press).

Cities of the United States: A Compilation of Current Information on Economic, Cultural, Geographical, and Social Conditions (Detroit, MI, 1994, Gale Research, Inc.).

Clifford, Denis, and Ralph Warner, *The Partnership Book* (Berkeley, CA 1991, Nolo Press).

Goldstein, Arnold S., *The Complete Guide to Buying and Selling a Business* (New York, 1983, Wiley).

Levinson, Jay Conrad, *Guerrilla Advertising: Cost-Effective Techniques for Small-Business Success* (Boston, 1994, Houghton Mifflin).

_____, and Bruce Jan Blechman, *Guerrilla Financing: Alternative Techniques to Finance Any Small Business* (Boston, MA, 1991, Houghton Mifflin).

_____ *Guerrilla Marketing: Secrets for Making Big Profits from Your Small Business* (Boston, MA, 2nd Ed. 1993, Houghton Mifflin).

_____ *Guerrilla Marketing Attack: New Strategies, Tactics & Weapons for Winning Big Profits from Your Small Business* (Boston, MA, 1989, Houghton Mifflin).

_____ *Guerrilla Marketing Excellence: The 50 Golden Rules for Small-Business Success* (Boston, 1993, Houghton Mifflin).

_____, and Seth Godin, *Guerrilla Marketing Handbook* (Boston, MA, 1994, Houghton Mifflin).

_____, and Charles Rubin, *Guerrilla Marketing Outline: The Entrepreneur's Guide to Earning Profits on the Internet* (Boston, MA, 1995, Houghton Mifflin).

_____ *Guerrilla Marketing Weapons: 100 Affordable Marketing Methods for Maximizing Profits from Your Small Business* (New York, 1990, Plume).

_____, Bill Gallagher, and Orvel Ray Wilson, *Guerrilla Selling: Unconventional Weapons and Tactics for Increasing Your Sales* (Boston, MA, 1992, Houghton Mifflin).

Retzler, Kathryn, *How to Start a Service Business and Make It Succeed* (Glenview, IL, 1987, Scott, Foresman & Co.).

Ross, Marilyn and Tom, *Big Marketing Ideas for Small Service Businesses* (Homewood, IL, 1990, Dow Jones-Irwin).

Savageau, David, and Richard Boyer, *Places Rated Almanac* (New York, 1993, Prentice Hall).

Steingold, Fred S., *Legal Guide for Starting and Running a Small Business* (Berkeley, CA, 1992, Nolo Press).

Stern, Linda, *Bookkeeping on Your Home-Based PC*, (New York, 1993, McGraw-Hill).

Tappan, William T., Jr., *Real Estate Exchange and Acquisition Techniques*, (Englewood Cliffs, NJ, 2nd ed., 1989, Prentice-Hall).

U.S. Department of Commerce, Bureau of the Census, *Statistical Abstract of the United States* (Washington, DC, 1992, U.S. Government Printing Office).

Webster, Bryce, *The Insider's Guide to Franchising* (New York, AMACOM, 1986).

State Boards of Accountancy*

**ALABAMA STATE BOARD OF PUB-
LIC ACCOUNTANCY**
 RSA Plaza
 770 Washington Avenue
 Montgomery, AL 36130
 Attn: Boyd E. Nicholson, Jr., CPA
  Executive Director
 Tel: (205) 242-5700
 Fax: (205) 242-2711

**ALASKA STATE BOARD OF PUBLIC
ACCOUNTANCY**
 Dept. of Commerce and Economic
Dev.
 Div. of Occ. Licensing, Box 110806
 Juneau, AK 99811-0806
 Attn: Steven Snyder
  Licensing Examiner
 Tel: (907) 465-2580
 Fax: (907) 255-1283

**ARIZONA STATE BOARD OF AC-
COUNTANCY**
 3110 North Nineteenth Avenue
 Suite 140
 Phoenix, AZ 85015-6038
 Attn: Ruth R. Lee
  Executive Director
 Tel: (602) 255-3648
 Fax: (602) 255-1283

**ARKANSAS STATE BOARD OF AC-
COUNTANCY**
 101 East Capitol, Suite 430
 Little Rock, AR 72201
 Attn: James E. Ward
  Executive Director
 Tel: (501) 682-1520
 Fax: (501) 682-5538

**CALIFORNIA STATE BOARD OF
ACCOUNTANCY**
 2135 Butano Drive, Suite 200
 Sacramento, CA 95825-0451
 Attn: Carol B. Sigmann
  Executive Director
 Tel: (916) 574-2155
 Fax: (916) 920-6547

**COLORADO STATE BOARD OF AC-
COUNTANCY**
 1560 Broadway, Suite 1370
 Denver, CO 80202
 Attn: Mary Lou Burgess
  Administrator
 Tel: (303) 894-7800
 Fax: (303) 894-7790

**CONNECTICUT STATE BOARD OF
ACCOUNTANCY**
 Secretary of the State
 30 Trinity Street
 Hartford, CT 06106
 Attn: David Guay
  Executive Director
 Tel: (203) 566-7835
 Fax: (203) 566-5757

**DELAWARE STATE BOARD OF AC-
COUNTANCY**
 Margaret O'Neill Building
 P.O. Box 1401
 Dover, DE 19903
 Attn: Sheila H. Wolfe
  Administrative Assistant
 Tel: (302) 739-4522
 Tax: (302) 739-6148

---

* *List of State Boards of Accountancy*, March 23, 1993, from the National Association of
State Boards of Accountancy, 380 Lexington Ave., New York, NY 10186-0002; (212) 490-
3868.

DISTRICT OF COLUMBIA BOARD OF ACCOUNTANCY

Dept. of Consumer & Reg. Aff., Rm 923
614 H Street, NW, c/o PO Box 37200
Washington, DC 20013-7200
Attn: Harriette E. Andrews
Board Representative
Tel: (202) 727-7468
Fax: (202) 727-8030

FLORIDA BOARD OF ACCOUNTANCY

2610 N.W. 43rd Street, Suite 1A
Gainseville, FL 32606
Attn: Martha P. Willis
Executive Director
Tel: (904) 336-2156
Fax: (904) 336-2164

GEORGIA STATE BOARD OF ACCOUNTANCY

166 Pryor Street, S.W.
Atlanta, GA 30303
Attn: Barbara Wilkerson
Executive Director
Tel: (404) 656-3941
Fax: (404) 651-9532

GUAM TERRITORIAL BOARD OF PUBLIC ACCOUNTANCY

KPMG Peat Marwick Bank of Guam Bldg.
Suite 800, 111 Chalan Santo Papa
Agana, GU 96910
Attn: Judith K. Borja, CPA
Chairman
Tel: (671) 472-2910
Fax: (671) 472-2918

HAWAII BOARD OF PUBLIC ACCOUNTANCY

Dept of Commerce & Consumer Affairs
P.O. Box 3469
Honolulu, HI 96801-3469
Attn: Verna Tomita
Executive Secretary
Tel: (808) 586-2694
Fax: (808) 586-2689

IDAHO STATE BOARD OF ACCOUNTANCY

Owyhee Plaza, Suite 470
11th & Main, Statehouse Mall
Boise, ID 83720
Attn: Brenda A. Blaszkiewicz
Executive Secretary
Tel: (208) 334-2490
Fax: (208) 334-2615

ILLINOIS COMMITTEE ON ACCOUNTANCY

University of IL Urbana-Champaign
10 Admin. Bldg., 506 S. Wright St
Urbana, IL 61801-3260
Attn: Linda Sergent
Secretary
Tel: (217) 333-1565
Fax: (217) 333-3126

ILLINOIS DEPARTMENT OF PROFESSIONAL REGULATION

Public Accountancy Section
320 W. Washington Street, 3rd floor
Springfield, IL 62786-0001
Attn: Judy Vargas
Manager
Tel: (217) 785-0800
Fax: (217) 782-7645

INDIANA STATE BOARD OF PUBLIC ACCOUNTANCY

Indiana Government Center North
100 North Senate Avenue
Indianapolis, IN 46204-2246
Attn: Sherrill Keesee
Administrative Assistant
Tel: (371) 232-3898
Fax: (317) 232-2312

IOWA ACCOUNTANCY EXAMINING BOARD

1918 S.E. Hulsizer Avenue
Ankeny, IA 50021
Attn: William M. Schroeder
Executive Secretary
Tel: (515) 281-4126
Fax: (515) 281-7372

KANSAS BOARD OF ACCOUNTANCY

Landon State Office Building
900 S.W. Jackson, Suite 556
Topeka, KS 66612-1239
Attn: Glenda S. Moore
   Executive Director
Tel: (913) 296-2162

KENTUCKY STATE BOARD OF ACCOUNTANCY

332 West Broadway, Suite 310
Louisville, KY 40202-2115
Attn: Susan G. Stopher
   Executive Director
Tel: (502) 595-3037
Fax: (502) 595-4281

STATE BOARD OF CPAS OF LOUISIANA

1515 World Trade Center
2 Canal Street
New Orleans, LA 70130
Attn: Mildred M. McGaha, CPA
   Executive Director
Tel: (504) 566-1244
Fax: (504) 566-1252

MAINE STATE BOARD OF ACCOUNTANCY

Dept. of Prof. & Fin. Reg., Div. of
Lic. & Enf., State House Station 35
Augusta, ME 04333
Attn: Sandy Leach
   Board Clerk
Tel: (207) 582-8723
Fax: (207) 582-5415

MARYLAND STATE BOARD OF PUBLIC ACCOUNTANCY

501 St. Paul Place, 9th floor
Baltimore, MD 21202-2272
Attn: Sue Mays
   Executive Director
Tel; (410) 333-6314
Fax: (410) 333-6314

MASSACHUSETTS STATE BOARD OF PUBLIC ACCOUNTANCY

Saltonstall Building, Room 1313
100 Cambridge Street
Boston, MA 02202-0001
Attn: Leo H. Bonarrigo, CPA
   Executive Secretary
Tel: (617) 727-1806
Fax: (617) 727-7378

MICHIGAN BOARD OF ACCOUNTANCY

Dept of Commerce - BOPR
P.O. Box 30018
Lansing, MI 48909-7518
Attn: Suzanne U. Jolicoeur
   Licensing Administrator
Tel: (517) 373-0682
Fax: (517) 373-2795

MINNESOTA STATE BOARD OF ACCOUNTANCY

85 East 7th Place
St. Paul, MN 55101
Attn: David O'Connell
   Executive Secretary
Tel: (612) 296-7937

MISSISSIPPI STATE BOARD OF PUBLIC ACCOUNTANCY

961 Highway 80 East, Suite A
Clinton, MS 39056-5246
Attn: Roy L. Horton, CPA
   Executive Director
Tel: (601) 924-8457

MISSOURI STATE BOARD OF ACCOUNTANCY

P.O. Box 613
Jefferson City, MO 65102-0613
Attn: William E. Boston, III
   Executive Director
Tel: (314) 751-0012
Fax: (314) 751-0890

MONTANA STATE BOARD OF PUB-LIC ACCOUNTANTS

Arcade Building, Lower Level
111 North Jackson
Helena, MT 59620-0407
Attn: Brenda St. Clair
   Administrator
Tel: (406) 444-3739
Fax: (406) 444-1667

NEBRASKA STATE BOARD OF PUB-LIC ACCOUNTANCY

P.O. Box 94725
Lincoln, NE 68509-4725
Attn: Marshall R. Whitlock
   Executive Director
Tel: (402) 471-3595
Fax: (402) 471-4484

NEVADA STATE BOARD OF AC-COUNTANCY

1 East Liberty Street, Suite 311
Reno, NV 89501-2110
Attn: William S. Zideck
   Executive Director
Tel: (702) 786-0231
Fax; (702) 786-0234

NEW HAMPSHIRE BOARD OF AC-COUNTANCY

57 Regional Drive
Concord, NH 03301
Attn: Louise O. MacMillan
   Assistant to the Board
Tel: (603) 271-3286

NEW JERSEY STATE BOARD OF ACCOUNTANCY

P.O. Box 45000
Newark, NJ 07101
Attn: John J. Meade
   Executive Director
Tel: (201) 504-6380
Fax: (201) 648-3536

NEW MEXICO STATE BOARD OF PUBLIC ACCOUNTANCY

1650 University N.E., Suite 400-A
Albuquerque, NM 87102
Attn: G. Trudy Beverley
   Executive Director
Tel: (505) 841-9109
Fax: (505) 841-9113

NEW YORK STATE BOARD FOR PUBLIC ACCOUNTANCY

State Education Department
Cultural Education Center, Rm 9A47
Albany, NY 12230-0001
Attn: Jean Fealy
   Administrator
Tel: (518) 474-3836
Fax: (518) 473-0578

NORTH CAROLINA STATE BOARD OF CPA EXAMINERS

1101 Oberlin Road, Suite 104
P.O. Box 12827
Raleigh, NC 27605-2827
Attn: Robert N. Brooks
   Executive Director
Tel: (919) 733-4222
Fax: (919) 733-4209

NORTH DAKOTA STATE BOARD OF ACCOUNTANCY

Box 8104, University Station
Grand Forks, ND 58202
Attn: Jim Abbott
   Executive Director
Tel: (701) 777-3869
Fax: (701) 777-3894

ACCOUNTANCY BOARD OF OHIO

77 South High Street, 18th floor
Columbus, OH 43266-0301
Attn: Timothy D. Haas
   Executive Director
Tel: (614) 466-4135
Fax: (614) 644-8112

OKLAHOMA ACCOUNTANCY BOARD

4545 Lincoln Blvd., Suite 165
Oklahoma City, OK 73105-3413
Attn: Diana Collinsworth
   Executive Director
Tel: (405) 521-2397
Fax: (405) 521-3118

OREGON STATE BOARD OF ACCOUNTANCY

158 12th Street, N.E.
Salem, OR 97310-0001
Attn: Karen DeLorenzo
   Administrator
Tel: (503) 378-4181
Fax: (503) 378-3575

PENNSYLVANIA STATE BOARD OF ACCOUNTANCY

613 Transportation & Safety Bldg.
P.O. Box 2649
Harrisburg, PA 17105-2649
Attn: J. Robert Kline
   Administrative Assistant
Tel: (717) 783-1404
Fax: (717) 787-7769

PUERTO RICO BOARD OF ACCOUNTANCY

Old San Juan Street
Box 3271
San Juan, PR 00904-3271
Attn: Luis A. Isaac Sanchez
   Director
Tel: (809) 722-2122
Fax: (809) 721-8399

RHODE ISLAND BOARD OF ACCOUNTANCY

Dept. of Business Regulation
233 Richmond Street, Suite 236
Providence, RI 02903-4236
Attn: Norma A. McLeod
   Executive Secretary
Tel: (401) 277-3185

SOUTH CAROLINA BOARD OF ACCOUNTANCY

Dutch Plaza, Suite 260
800 Dutch Square Blvd.
Columbia SC 29210
Attn: Fred E. Stuart, CPA
   Director
Tel: (803) 731-1677
Fax: (803) 731-1680

SOUTH DAKOTA BOARD OF ACCOUNTANCY

301 East 14th Street, Suite 200
Sioux Falls, SD 57104
Attn: Lynn J. Bethke
   Executive Director
Tel: (605) 339-6746

TENNESSEE STATE BOARD OF ACCOUNTANCY

500 James Robertson Parkway
2nd floor
Nashville, TN 37219
Attn: Don Hummel
   Director of Administration
Tel: (615) 741-2550
Fax: (615) 741-6470

TEXAS STATE BOARD OF PUBLIC ACCOUNTANCY

1033 La Posada, Suite 340
Austin, TX 78752-3892
Attn: William Treacy
   Executive Director
Tel: (512) 451-0241
Fax: (512) 450-7075

UTAH BOARD OF ACCOUNTANCY

160 East 300 South
P.O. Box 45802
Salt Lake City, UT 84145-0802
Attn: James B. Adamson
   Administrator
Tel: (801) 530-6456
Fax: (801) 530-6511

VERMONT BOARD OF PUBLIC ACCOUNTANCY
Pavilion Office Bldg.
Montpelier, VT 05609-1106
Attn: Loris Rollins
Staff Assistant
Tel: (802) 828-2837
Fax: (802) 828-2496

VIRGINIA BOARD FOR ACCOUNTANCY
3600 West Broad Street
Richmond, VA 23230-4917
Attn: Robert L. Banning
Assistant Director
Tel: (804) 367-8505
Fax: (804) 367-2475

VIRGIN ISLANDS BOARD OF PUBLIC ACCOUNTANCY
1B King Street
Christiansted
St. Croix, VI 00820-4933
Attn: Alan Bronstein, CPA
Secretary
Tel: (809) 773-0096
Fax: (809) 778-8640

WASHINGTON STATE BOARD OF ACCOUNTANCY
210 East Union, Suite H
P.O. Box 9131
Olympia, WA 98507-9131
Attn: Carey L. Rader, CPA
Executive Director
Tel: (206) 753-2585
Fax: (206) 664-9190

WEST VIRGINIA BOARD OF ACCOUNTANCY
201 L & S Building
812 Quarrier Street
Charleston, WV 25301-2617
Attn: JoAnn Walker
Executive Secretary
Tel: (304) 558-3557

WISCONSIN ACCOUNTING EXAMINING BOARD
1400 E. Washington Avenue
P.O. Box 8935
Madison, WI 53708-8935
Attn: Peter T. Eggert
Bureau Director
Tel: (608) 266-1397
Fax: (608) 267-0644

WYOMING BOARD OF CERTIfiED PUBLIC ACCOUNTANTS
Barrett Building, 2nd floor
Room 217-218
Cheyenne, WY 82002
Attn: Peggy Morgando
Executive Director
Tel: (307) 777-7551
Fax: (307) 777-6005

Professional Associations

American Institute of Professional Bookkeepers
6001 Montrose Road, Suite 207
Rockville, MD 20852
Telephone: (800) 622-0121

40,000 members. Dues $60. Dedicated to providing tax and professional practice advice for bookkeepers. Offers continuing professional education courses, fax or overnight delivery of any federal or state tax form; membership discounts on express mail; free telephone hotline consultation; group errors and omissions insurance; reduced rates on publications. One notable recent publication is *The Encyclopedia of Journal Entries*, which is the mother of all master charts of accounts. Monthly newsletter *The General Ledger*; quarterly, *The Journal of Accounting, Taxation and Finance for Business*.

American Society of Tax Professionals
P.O. Box 1024
Sioux Falls, SD 57101
Telephone: (605) 335-1185

Founded 1987; 250 members; staff 1. Member controlled and operated. Dues $65. For tax preparers, enrolled agents, public accountants, certified public accountants, attorneys. Offers 16 hours of continuing professional education at reduced fee. Referral to members with expertise in special problem areas. Group errors and omission insurance; group health insurance. Issuance of news releases concerning members. Bimonthly newsletter, *Tax Professional's Update*.

Institute of Certified Financial Planners
7600 East Eastman Avenue, Suite 301
Denver, CO 80231
Telephone: (303) 751-7600; (800) 322-4237; Fax: (303) 751-1037

Founded in 1973; members 7,800; staff 20. Members are people who have been designated Certified Financial Planners (CFPs), business professionals in the financial planning industry, and those who are enrolled in programs accredited by the International Board of Standards and Practices for Certified Financial Planners. It seeks to establish and maintain professionalism in financial planning; and to provide a forum for the exchange of ideas; to insure the integrity of continuing education programs. It conducts regional conference and advertising programs and maintains a referral service.

Its publications include the bimonthly *Institute of Certified Financial Planners' CFP Today*, and the quarterly *Journal of Financial Planning*.

National Association of Enrolled Agents
6000 Executive Boulevard, Suite 205
Rockville, MD 20852
Telephone (301) 984-6232; (800) 424-4339; Fax: (301) 231-8961

Founded 1972. Membership 7,000, staff 10. An association of individuals who have acquired EA status and are qualified to represent all classes of taxpayers at any administrative level of the Internal Revenue Service. It promotes ethical representation of taxpayers' financial position before government agencies, and conducts seminars and conferences to keep members informed of legislation and regulations affecting the profession.

It also makes presentations to civic, community, educational, and employee groups to inform the public of its rights, privileges, and obligations under tax laws and regulations. It conducts the National Tax Practice Institute, a three-year program in taxpayer representation and audit procedures. Its computer services include a database of enrolled agent mailing lists.

Publications include a quarterly, *Enrolled Agent*, and *EAlert*, a newsletter. Its annual meetings are always in August.

National Association of Tax Practitioners
720 Association Drive
Appleton, WI 54914
Telephone: (800) 558-3402; WI (800) 242-3430; Fax: (800) 747-0001.

Founded 1979. Dues $75; with application add $15. 14,000 members; staff 26. For people engaged in preparation of federal or state tax returns, including tax preparers, enrolled agents, accountants, licensed public accountants, CPAs and attorneys.

State chapters. Toll-free research center and state assistance volunteers. Two- or three-day nationwide workshops for continuing professional education (CPE) credits (8 CPE credits per day). Annual national conference. Professional insurance programs for professional liability errors and omissions in all 50 states, business coverage, life, accidental death and dismemberment, medical and individual disability income, including office overhead. Discounts on personal and business car rentals, hotel savings program, credit card. IRS forms, out-of-state forms, bookstore, tax-related supplies & services, client newsletters and brochures, *Tax Practitioners Journal*, *1040 Report*, monthly newsletter.

If you find yourself in a very specialized practice and want the support of a specialized professional group, consult the *Encyclopedia of Associations* at your local public library.

Franchises

If you want an **H&R Block** franchise you will probably have to buy it from an existing franchisee. A telephone call [(816) 753-6900] to Block's corporate headquarters (410 Main Street, Kansas City, MO 64111) gets a message that the company is just about franchised out and not opening any new stores.

Triple Check (727 South Main Street, Burbank, CA 91508, telephone (818) 840-9078) has three franchise options—Tax Preparation, Business Consulting, and Financial Planning. A franchisee can combine any or all, or use just one. There is no start-up fee and no royalty on existing clients, because it is "conversion franchise" for building established practitioners' businesses. Calculated by gross earnings and number of returns, royalties compare well with others in the industry. Besides regional meetings, there is an annual meeting at year's end with seminars on tax laws, rules, cases, and business and professional practice. Advertising is tailored for the licensee who buys only space in local media. Credits for CPE apply to state certification programs and for CPA requirements.

E.K. Williams & Co., a subsidiary of the Dwyer Group (1010 N. University Parks Dr., P.O. Box 3146, Waco, TX 76707, telephone (800) 583-9100), began franchising in 1947. It offers information and business management services that address small businesses' needs. Franchise fees are $40,000 to $50,000, with a $65,000 to $75,000 total investment.

Franchisees of **General Business Services**, another Dwyer Group subsidiary, provides business management, financial, and tax counseling, as well as personnel services. The franchise fee is $30,000 to $40,000, with a total investment from $35,000 to $45,000, and royalties from 2% to 8%.

The Dwyer Group offers licensees two-week initial and continuing training, provides a business operating system, business and tax libraries, and marketing assistance. Seminars provide accreditation toward EA, CPA, and CFP designations.

Jackson Hewitt Tax Service (4575 Bonney Road, Virginia Beach, VA 23462, telephone (800) 234-3278) provides training, operating manual, proprietary software to maximize deductions and reduce mathematical errors, electronic filing for SuperFast Refund, business management training, tax school, staff over 100. Franchise fee $17,500 to $20,000, total investment $29,920 to $44,600; royalty 12% of gross volume after discounts, advertising 6% of gross volume after discounts.

See also Bryce Webster's *Insider's Guide to Franchising* and Dennis L. Foster's *Rating Guide to Franchises* cited in the bibliography. Among standard directories try *The Franchise Annual Handbook & Directory* (St. Catherines, Ontario, Info Press) and the *Franchise Opportunities Handbook* (Washington, DC, latest ed., U.S. Dept. of Commerce).

Software

LaCerte software dominates this business. But don't take my word for it. Look around. The best way to acquire professional accounting and tax software is to read the trade journals and get the demo disks. Software changes so fast that only periodicals give a sense of the market. Here are a few more professional programs.

TAASCforce from Tax & Accounting Software Corp. (6914 South Yorktown Ave., Tulsa, OK 74136, (800) 998-9990) offers its *EasyACCT Professional Series*, bundled or not with *Professional Tax System*. They make up an integrated set designed by CPAs on 29 floppy disks or two CD-ROMs. Tax modules integrate federal and state programs, permit instant summaries from any screen for "what if" calculations, include supporting forms and schedules, and have automatic rollover from prior years. *EasyACCT* is designed to serve client needs in an integrated system by switching between modules. Data entered in one module appears in related modules. At press time the whole package listed for $1490. It is often discounted and available on a trial basis, and you can have the prior year tax modules on CD-ROM free.

Solomon IV, from Solomon Software (200 East Hardin Street, P.O. Box 414, Findlay, OH 45839-0414, telephone (800) SOLOMON) is the Nimitz class of accounting software. Purchasing a license to use the basic module for $2,995 gets you a 3-day training seminar and the right to hire Development Resource Center personnel's services to customize the program. While possibly exceeding your immediate needs, it will no doubt handle anything else conceivable.

Veritax 1040 for Windows (Veritax, 4420 Varsity Drive, Ann Arbor, MI 48108; (800) 837-4829). This company's CD-ROM for $295 includes all federal forms and schedules with worksheets, with built-in instructions, calculation, and electronic filing features.

CPSystems, Inc. (P.O. Box 81226, Boca Raton, FL 83481; (800) 446-0063) offers a tax form service on CD-ROM which includes federal forms, the forms for all 50 states, or 10 states in any region of the country, and selected municipal tax forms. Prices range from $495 for the whole federal-state-local package to $195 for federal forms or 10 states' forms. Available in DOS or Windows versions, includes schedules with worksheet, built-in instructions, calculation, and electronic filing.

Good accounting programs in the consumer market launch overwhelmingly from Windows. We note the following with no promises or guarantees. Shown are *street prices*, those I found discounted by a popular mail-order retailer. Contact the publishers for demonstration disks or literature. I omit most tax and accounting software on the market today, as most will be gone tomorrow.

QuickBooks Pro (Intuit Corporation P.O. Box 3014, Menlo Park, CA 94026; telephone (800) 624-8742, about $200, discounted), now Windows only, is my (DOS) basic bookkeeping tool. It handles all but the most complex jobs. Intuit's products are simple, powerful, and cheap. **Peachtree Complete Accounting, Ver. 9.0** and **Peachtree Accounting, Ver. 3.5** (Peachtree Software, 1505 Pavilion Place, Norcross, GA 30093; (800) 554-8900, about $200 & $120, discounted). A venerable and competitive full-featured accounting program, it handles multi-department corporations and offers payroll and client write-up modules. **Timeslips** (Timeslips Corp., 239 Western Ave., Essex, MA 01929 (508) 768-6100, about $200 discounted) helps you bill hourly.

CD-ROMs and On-line Services

CD-ROMs

There are now three major tax data sources and one peripheral player on CD-ROM. Tax Management, Inc., is a subsidiary of the **Bureau of National Affairs** (BNA), 1250 23rd Street, NW, Washington, DC 20037-1166; (800) 372-1033. Provides a Tax Practice Series on CD-ROM for planning and compliance, accessible by key-word searches; *Tax Management Portfolios* on CD-ROM comprises over 250 portfolio volumes of specialized tax topics,including Federal income, estates, gifts & trusts, and foreign income. Both series analyze and research individual topics. The disks are updated monthly. It is $2,200 per year, Windows or DOS.

Commerce Clearing House's *ProSystem fx*, (Windows or DOS) is available on cd-rom or on-line, and the same commands operate both systems. Disks are updated monthly; annual service is from $1,143 for the *SmartPLANNER* to $2,089 for the Federal Tax Reporters. CCH, 4025 West Peterson Ave., Chicago, IL 60646; (800) TELL CCH (835-5224), mailbox no. 1328, will get you a sales rep.

Research Institute of America (RIA), 90 Fifth Avenue, New York, NY 10011 (800) 431-9025, Ext.3, provides the following CD-ROMs for DOS or Windows, *On Point System*, a tax research and compliance library of basic and advanced tax materials updated monthly; *State and Local Taxes*, statutes, cases, rulings, updated monthly; *Tax Advisors Planning System*, written and updated monthly by a network of expert practitioners, covering 30 major topics; *Tax Desk* a research and compliance system for individuals, and closely held businesses; and *Tax Guide Plus*, core tax research tools on one CD—tens of thousands of pages of research materials related by smart links. Prices are available on inquiry.

The peripheral player, **Warren, Gorham & Lamont**, The Park Square Building, 31 St. James Avenue, Boston, MA 02116-4112; (800) 950-1210, ext. 8350, has transferred its major treatises, including *International Taxation*, *Estate Planning Taxation*, and *Business Entities Taxation*, to one CD-ROM. Buy one, you have them all and can pay as you need them.

On-line

As noted elsewhere, BNA and RIA tax services are available on-line via the **Lexis-Nexis** library. If you expand your references resources, you will have to compare carefully to decide whether to use the CD-ROMs or go on-line. The only major service not available now on Lexis-Nexis is *CCH ACCESS*.

You can subscribe to the Nexis side of the service on a pay-as-you-go basis. Total costs under this plan depend on the level and frequency of use. Currently pay-as-you-do requires a $50 monthly account fee, plus 65¢ a minute for on-line time, $6.00 to $50.00 for file access, and $1.00 to $45.00 to download or print out a document. Lexis-Nexis recommends beginning with the flat rate to learn the electronic ropes while keeping costs down. The $500 monthly flat rate includes the $50 account fee, on-line time, file access, and document downloading. Depending on use it may or may not be a bargain. The number for information about the services is (800) 426-7675.

Commerce Clearing House's *CCH ACCESS Online*. CCH Computax, Inc., Worldwide Postal Center, P.O. Box 92938, Los Angeles, CA 90009; (800) 248-3248 is available for a $250 registration fee and a fee for the first two hours at $100/hour. For the $450 you get user's guide, user ID, software and an hour's free training time that you must use in the first 30 days. Billing thereafter is in hourly increments. As the only major tax service not available on Lexis-Nexis is Commerce Clearing House's *CCH ACCESS* compares favorably with the others, and, while restricted to CCH reports alone, is cheaper. If, on the other hand, you require a wide-ranging on-line search, you may prefer the Nexis universe.

INITIAL INVESTMENT REQUIREMENTS

ITEM	Quote No. 1	Quote No. 2	Quote No. 3
Furnishings and office equipment			
Office:			
Desk & chair	$_____	$_____	$_____
Desk lamp (optional)	_____	_____	_____
Customer chairs	_____	_____	_____
Computer table or desk	_____	_____	_____
Storage & file cabinets	_____	_____	_____
Telephone	_____	_____	_____
Typewriter (noncmputer forms)	_____	_____	_____
Plants, artwork	_____	_____	_____
Reception:			
Desk & chair (if have assistant)	$_____	$_____	$_____
Telephone (if have assistant)	_____	_____	_____
Couch (optional)	_____	_____	_____
Arm chairs	_____	_____	_____
End table	_____	_____	_____
Lamps, art, plants, etc.	_____	_____	_____
Storage			
File cabinets	$_____	$_____	$_____
Shelving	_____	_____	_____
"Bankers" boxes	_____	_____	_____
Professional equipment & supplies			
Day-date calendar (2 if have assistant)	$_____	$_____	$_____
Business cards & stationery	_____	_____	_____
Printing calculator	_____	_____	_____
Desk-top supplies & equipment	_____	_____	_____
File folders and clips	_____	_____	_____
Laser paper, yellow pads, post-its, etc.	_____	_____	_____
Pens, pencils, paper clips, etc.	_____	_____	_____
Licenses, permits, fees			
Permits	$_____	$_____	$_____
Business license	_____	_____	_____
State registration fees	_____	_____	_____
SUBTOTAL:	$_____	$_____	$_____

START-UP COST ESTIMATES

These two pages listing start-up costs can be enlarged up to 182% for 8½x11-inch worksheets. Quoted prices can be arranged in order of their receipt or set out as high, middle, and low prices. They will also help organize the start-up process. Remember always to balance cost with value.

INITIAL INVESTMENT REQUIREMENTS (Continued)

ITEM	Quote No. 1	Quote No. 2	Quote No. 3
Computer equipment			
Fast, big, high-quality computer, with:	$_____	$_____	$_____
4x to 6x CD-ROM drive	_____	_____	_____
Fax-modem (high-end features)	_____	_____	_____
1- to 2-megabyte video card	_____	_____	_____
Large, good-quality monitor	_____	_____	_____
Tape back-up & software	_____	_____	_____
Accounting & tax prep programs	_____	_____	_____
Fast, high-resolution laser printer	_____	_____	_____
Copier for quick, back-up work (optional)	$_____	$_____	$_____
Building or Leasehold renovation and decoration			
Architect or contractor design work	$_____	$_____	$_____
Carpentry, electric, plumbing, painting,	_____	_____	_____
carpeting costs			
Telephone line installations	_____	_____	_____
Signs & exterior work	_____	_____	_____
On-line sign-up fees	$_____	$_____	$_____
Pre-opening expenses			
Rent advances and security deposits	$_____	$_____	$_____
Utility security deposits	_____	_____	_____
Insurance fees	_____	_____	_____
Freight charges	_____	_____	_____
Professional fees & commissions			
Lawyer	$_____	$_____	$_____
Insurance broker	_____	_____	_____
Real estate broker	_____	_____	_____
On-line sign-up fees	$_____	$_____	$_____
Miscellaneous	$_____	$_____	$_____
(e.g., assistant's equipment & supplies	_____	_____	_____
TOTAL	$_____	$_____	$_____

START-UP COST ESTIMATES, CONTINUED

MARKET SURVEY
Questionnaire

Date: _____

Company Name: _____

Telephone Number: _____

Contact Name: _____

1. Fee Structure:

   Hourly? ___Yes ___No; How Much Per Hour?_____

   If Per Unit: What Units?*_____ How Much Per Unit?_____*

2. Tax Preparation Fees:

   Average Individual Return: State: _____; Federal _____

   Average Business Return: _____

   Partnership: _____

   Corporation: _____

3. Write-Up Work:

   Hourly Rate: _____

*Comments:_____

_____

_____

_____

_____

_____

_____

MARKET SURVEY QUESTIONNAIRE

If you can copy this form at a 182% enlargement, it will make a full 8½x11-inch worksheet.

The average work year has about 2,000 hours (40 hours per week times 50 weeks). Not all are billable hours. Subtract for holidays and for administrative, promotional, and (yes) wasted time. Add for days exceeding eight hours. Your projected average hourly rate (based on your market survey) times estimated or desired *billable* hours is the year's potential gross income. *Hourly cost* of doing business equals Total Operation Cost from the Profit and Loss spreadsheet divided by your *projected* billable hours.

Comparing the gross income calculation to the cost calculation should show the feasibility of your plan.

PROFIT & LOSS SPREADSHEET ITEMS

INCOME:
EXPENSES:
  FIXED EXPENSES:
      Rent or mortgage payments
      Start-up loan repayment
      Interest on any loans
      Utilities
         Telephone basic fees
         Electricity
         Gas
         Water & sewerage
         Trash pickup
      Staff salaries (if any)
      Janitorial services
      Taxes, licenses, permits
      Security
      Advertising & promotion
      Insurance
      Professional fees
      Software updates & on-line fees
      Professional dues subscriptions
      Reception-room subscriptions
      Cost recovery (depreciation)
  VARIABLE EXPENSES:
      Batch or modem form-processing
      Telephone use fees
      On-line use fees
      Temporary help
      Copying
      Supplies
TOTAL PRACTICE EXPENSES:
  LESS:
      Living expenses
      Profit
NET CASH POSITION:
CUMULATIVE CASH POSITION:

Any or all the above items may be used to set up a profit and loss spreadsheet for your proposed business. Enter each that applies and extend it for 12 months and a year-end total.

GENERAL INFORMATION & DISCLOSURE BROCHURE
(FINANCIAL PLANNING)

Gordon P. Lewis & Company
Registered Investment Advisor
125 Second Street
Lakeport, CA 95453
(707) 263-9288

Gordon P. Lewis has been registered with the U.S. Securities and Exchange
Commission (S.E.C.) and the State of California Department of Corporations as a R.I.A. since 1994.

PERSONNEL
Gordon P. Lewis has been engaged in the Income Tax Preparation and
Financial Planning Business since 1978. Mr. Lewis is licensed by the State
of California to sell Life, Health, Disability, and Variable Insurance Products (1986). He is also a General Securities Registered Representative (series
7, 1996).

HOW I OPERATE
For a fee, negotiable in the range of $100 per hour and payable after the
consultations, I will give you advice on your financial concerns, including,
but not limited to: investments, budgeting, and bill paying, divorce settle-
ments, money worries, retirement planning, what not to do financially, credit
counseling, insurance planning, inheritances, college funding, and general
tax planning.

You are the sole determiner of how many hours of financial counseling you
will need. You may continue for as long as you think it is necessary or you
can stop any time.

If you wish to implement my advice by purchasing securities or insurance
products, you are free to select any brokers you wish. However, if you wish
me to implement the advice, my securities broker, first Associated Securities
Group, or my insurance companies, ITT Hartford, among others, or my Tax
Preparation Service will be recommended. I will earn the normal sales
commissions on any transactions placed through them. Any commission
earned will be credited toward the hourly fee. Lower fees for comparable
services may be available from other sources.

GENERAL INFORMATION
Most of my clients are individuals, but I also work with pension funds,
trusts & estates, and businesses. I give advice on all securities, ranging from
government bonds to commodities. I do not do security analysis—I rely on
broker/dealer and mutual fund recommendations. My main sources of
financial information are financial magazines & newspapers, research
materials provided by others, corporate rating services and company reports
& press releases. My investment strategy is investing for the long term. On
occasion I may buy or sell securities for myself that I recommend to clients.
There is no conflict of interest as the securities are widely-held and publicly
traded. I review client accounts quarterly, on a portfolio analysis basis. I do
not prepare regular reports for clients, the broker/dealer and mutual funds

do. I do not do anything without client consent. And I do not compensate, directly or indirectly, anyone for client referrals.

ACKNOWLEDGMENTS
This is to acknowledge that I/we have read and understood the GENERAL INFORMATION & DISCLOSURE STATEMENT of Gordon P. Lewis, Registered Investment Advisor. I/we agree to pay an hourly fee of $_____ for financial planning advice, payable at the conclusion of each session.

X_____

X_____

Street _____

City, State, Zip _____

Home phone _____ Work phone_____

This is to acknowledge receipt of $_____ for financial planning services.

X_____
Gordon P. Lewis   Date
Registered Investment Advisor

Gordon P. Lewis & Company
125 Second Street
Lakeport, CA 95453

(707) 263-9288

This Financial Planning Agreement is entered into on this _____ day of
_____, 199___, by and between Gordon P. Lewis & Company
(hereinafter referred to as "PLANNER") AND _____

(hereinafter referred to as "CLIENT").

WHEREAS PLANNER is registered with the Securities and Exchange
Commission under the Investment Act of 1940 and is registered with the
Department of Corporations for the State of California as an Investment
Advisor; and

WHEREAS CLIENT wishes to retain PLANNER to help assess CLIENT's
assets and liabilities; present and foreseeable financial obligations; and
present and potential income in relation to CLIENT's financial goals;

NOW, THEREFORE, in consideration of the foregoing, the parties hereto
agree as follows:

 PLANNER agrees to consult with CLIENT for the purpose of acquiring
information pertinent to the considerations described above and CLIENT
agrees to provide such information and data as PLANNER requires.

PLANNER hereby notifies CLIENT that Gordon P. Lewis, sole proprietor
of PLANNER, is also a Registered Representative with first Associated
Securities Group, Member NASD, SIPC. In such capacity Lewis receives
transaction income from the buying and selling of securities. Lewis is also
licensed with the State of California as a Life Insurance Agent. This dual
capacity may result in a conflict of interest between PLANNER and CLI-
ENT.

PLANNER hereby notifies CLIENT that CLIENT is under no obligation to
act upon any of the specific recommendations made by PLANNER; and that
should CLIENT elect to act upon any specific recommendation of PLAN-
NER, CLIENT is not obligated to effect such transaction(s) through PLAN-
NER.

As compensation to PLANNER for rendering the financial Planning described above, CLIENT agrees to pay PLANNER at a negotiable rate of
$100 per hour after a complimentary first hour of consultation. This fee will
be accumulated and billed by PLANNER to CLIENT in increments of $100
for time already expended. CLIENT agrees to remit payment within 10 days
of receipt of PLANNER's bill.

CLIENT acknowledges that lower fees for comparable services may be
available from other sources.

PLANNER makes no promises, warranties, guarantees or representations that its services will result in profit to CLIENT or in CLIENT's meeting his/her financial objectives.

CLIENT acknowledges receipt of a copy of the information contained in Part II of Form ADV as required under Rule 204-3 of the Investment Advisors Act of 1940.

PLANNER agrees not to assign its rights or delegate its duties under this agreement without the express written consent of CLIENT.

This financial Planning Agreement may be terminated by CLIENT or PLANNER upon written notice to the other party; cancellation does not relieve CLIENT of obligation to pay PLANNER for time already expended.

JOINT AND SEVERAL OBLIGATIONS; in the event more than one person executes this agreement as CLIENT, each person signing as CLIENT hereby agrees to be jointly and severally bound by each obligation assumed by CLIENT hereunder.

CLIENT hereby agrees to the provisions of this agreement on the date first above stated.

Telephone Number	CLIENT Signature	Date
	Citizenship	Birth Date
Telephone Number	CLIENT Signature	Date
	Citizenship	Birth Date
	CLIENT Street Address	
	City State ZIP	
	CLIENT Mailing Address	
	City State ZIP	

ADVISOR hereby agrees to the provisions of this agreement, effective as of the _____ of _____, 199___.

ADVISOR's Signature	Date

```
                    CONSUMER CREDIT COUNSELING INTAKE SHEET

         CLIENT                        SPOUSE
         Name: _____       Name: _____
         SSN: _____ - ___ - _____      SSN: _____ - ___ - _____
         Address:_____        Address: _____
         _____
         Phone No.:_____        Phone No.: _____
         Occupation:_____         Spouse's Occupation:_____
         Employer:_____         Spouse's Employer:_____
         Address:_____         Address: _____
         _____
         Phone No: _____         Phone No.: _____
         Dependents:
         Name _____    Age _____  Relationship _____
         Name _____    Age _____  Relationship _____
         Name _____    Age _____  Relationship _____
         Name _____    Age _____  Relationship _____
```

```
                                            CLIENT        SPOUSE
         INCOME
         Monthly income after all deductions:
            Salary                           $_____      $_____
            Other income                     _____       _____
                                             _____       _____

            TOTAL INCOME:                    $_____

         EXPENSES
         Rent/Mortgage:                      $_____
            Taxes $_____ Ins. $_____ (incl?)  _____
         Utilities
            Electricity:                     _____
            Heating fuel:                    _____
            Water & sewer:                   _____
            Telephone:                       _____
            Garbage:                         _____
            Other utilities:                 _____
         Home maintenance:                   _____
         Food:                               _____
         Clothing:                           _____
         Laundry & dry cleaning:             _____
         Medical & dental expenses:          _____
         Transportation (excl. car pmts.):   _____
         Recreation, clubs, entertainment:   _____
         Insurance
            Homeowners (if not already above): _____
            Health:                          _____
            Auto:                            _____
            Other insurance:                 _____
         Taxes not in payroll or mortgage
            (describe:_____)        _____
         Other (describe:_____)     _____

            TOTAL EXPENSES:                  $_____
```

The forms on the following three pages relating to consumer credit counseling can be increasesd 182 percent for use as 8½x11" documents. Or you may customize the formats to your own needs.

CONSUMER CREDIT COUNSELING INTAKE - PAGE 2

Credit Cards
Account Name   Account No. Current Balance   Int. Rate   Min. Mthly. Pmt
_____   _____ $_____   _____ $_____
_____   _____ $_____   _____ $_____
_____   _____ $_____   _____ $_____
_____   _____ $_____   _____ $_____
_____   _____ $_____   _____ $_____
_____   _____ $_____   _____ $_____

Other Accounts
Account Name   Account No. Current Balance   Int. Rate   Min. Mthly. Pmt
_____   _____ $_____   _____ $_____
_____   _____ $_____   _____ $_____
_____   _____ $_____   _____ $_____
_____   _____ $_____   _____ $_____

Mortgage(s):
Curent Balance: $_____   Monthly Pmt $_____   Int. Rate _____
                 $_____ $_____   _____
                 $_____ $_____   _____

Auto Loan(s):
Curent Balance: $_____   Monthly Pmt $_____   Int. Rate _____
                 $_____ $_____   _____
                 $_____ $_____   _____
DMV Renewals: $_____
                 $_____

PROPERTY OWNED   Value   Value
Real Estate   Cash
  Dwelling $_____   Cash on Hand $_____
  Condominium   _____   Checking Acct*   _____
  Time Share   _____   Savings Acct*   _____
  Co-op Apt   _____   CDs   _____
  Commercial   _____   T-Bills   _____
  Rental Ppty   _____   Money Mkt Acct   _____
  Land   _____   Brokerage Acct   _____
  Other   _____   Other   _____

Personal Property   Security Investments
  Automobile(s) $_____   Common Stock $_____
                 _____   Preferred Stock   _____
  Furniture   _____   Corp. Bonds   _____
  Appliances   _____   Tax-exempt Bonds _____
  Jewelry   _____   U.S. Svgs Bonds   _____
  Art   _____   Mutual Funds   _____
  Antiques   _____   Other   _____
  Computer   _____
  Other   _____

*Existing Bank Accounts: Institution Name & Address   Account No.
_____   #_____
_____   #_____
_____   #_____
_____   #_____

   The foregoing information correctly states my/our financial obligations and assets. Any change in the above information or will be added
by my/our signed written statement.
Signed _____   Date_____
Signed _____   Date_____

CREDIT COUNSELING GOAL SHEET

This is a brief contract that allows us to set up goals in the order of their priority. (e.g., 1. get out of debt; 2. start a savings account; 3. establish an investment plan; etc.)

1._____

2._____

3._____

4._____

5._____

6._____

7._____

8._____

This list will be a starting place. We will re-evaluate it as needed, and as we meet the goals. It is very important for you to know what your goals are. The counseling process will require self-discipline and some sacrifice. Knowing where you want to go will make the process much more tolerable.

You agree to surrender to CREDIT COUNSELOR all credit cards that you have not already destroyed, and you will forward all income when you receive it to CREDIT COUNSELOR for distribution. As compensation for setting up and administering the credit plan, you agree to pay CREDIT COUNSELOR at the rate of $75 per hour. CREDIT COUNSELOR will withdraw such compensation from the income you forward and will note it in the monthly statement to you.

Dated _____, 199__   Gordon P. Lewis & Company

                                      by   _____
                                           CREDIT COUNSELOR

Agreed to by

_____
(signed)

_____
(signed)

on _____, 199___.

Index

Copy this page to order from

ACTON CIRCLE—

Bookkeeping and Tax Preparation: Start and Build a Prosperous Bookkeeping, Tax, and Financial Services Business, by Gordon P. Lewis.
The techniques and information you need to build your flair for figures into a highly profitable, well-rounded business. 179 pages, 7x10", index, bibliog., forms; $18.95.

The Baker's Trade: A Recipe for Creating the Successful Small Bakery, by Zachary Y. Schat
All you need to know for starting and managing a retail or wholesale bakery that's in tune with today's changing tastes. 275 pages, 8½x11", illus., appendixes, bibliog.; $24.95.

Lawn Care & Gardening: A Down-to-Earth Guide to the Business, by Kevin Rossi.
Everything about soils, fertilizers, grasses, plants, pests, tools, techniques, and good business practices to make a landscaping business pay. Reproducible forms. 220 pages, 8½x11", illus., index, bibliog.; $21.95.

The Poison Ivy, Oak & Sumac Book: A Short Natural History and Cautionary Account, by Thomas E. Anderson.
Color photographs of each of these noxious plants in different seasons. Little-known historical, medical, and botanical facts. Recognize and avoid the plants to prevent a rash, or learn how to cope if you couldn't avoid them. 130 pages, 6x9", illus., index, bibliog.; $14.95.

Send your check or money order to
Acton Circle Publishing Co.
P.O. Box 1564
Ukiah, CA 95482

Enclosed is $_____ for _____ copy(ies) of

_____ $_____

and $_____ for _____ copy(ies) of

_____ $_____

Shipping/Handling ($1.50 1st book; $0.75 others)* $_____

CA residents add 7.25% sales tax $_____

Total $_____

Name_____

Street_____Apt._____

City_____State_____ZIP_____

*Or Postal First Class at $3.00 per book.

You may return any book for a full refund, no questions asked.

Copy this page to order